D1134676

ANCIENT JORDAN FROM THE AIR

David Kennedy and Robert Bewley

DEDICATION

To Julie and to Jill, who have been deeply involved in our passion for flying and archaeology for a generation.

ANCIENT JORDAN FROM THE AIR

David Kennedy and Robert Bewley

London 2004

Published by
The Council for British Research in the Levant
The British Academy
10 Carlton House Terrace
London, SW1Y 5AH

British Library Cataloguing in Publication Data
A catalogue record for this book is available from the British Library
ISBN 0-9539102-2-9

This book is available from Oxbow Books, Park End Place, Oxford, OX1 1HN

Typeset by Meeks & Middleton
Printed in Britain by Henry Ling Ltd, Dorset

CONTENTS

PREFACE AND ACKNOWLEDGEMENTS

THE genesis of this book lies in the 1970s and in the impact, on the young students we then were, of two books. Père Antoine Poidebard's magnificent *La trace de Rome dans le désert de Syrie* (1934) was one; Raymond Schoder's *Ancient Greece from the Air* (1974) was the other. The idea for a similar book to Schoder's for the archaeology of Jordan, was first considered a few years later but remained unattainable for some 25 years. In 1997 events took a positive turn. Wing Commander Mike Sedman was Air Attaché at the British Embassy in Amman at that time and although admitting he had scant interest in archaeology, he nevertheless insisted on the importance of the flying programme envisaged. Existing support and patronage from the then Crown Prince El-Hassan, was complemented by Mike Sedman who secured an interview for Kennedy with Colonel Prince Feisal (now Brigadier General and Commander of the Royal Jordanian Air Force). Prince Feisal in turn arranged for a flight the next day and agreed to more in 1998 and 1999. Further flying has been possible every year since, either with private companies or the RJAF. Naturally our first and overwhelmingly important debt is to these three supporters and facilitators. We are deeply indebted to both Their Royal Highnesses. In view of what we have to say about pioneering work by the RAF in Transjordan in the 1920s, it is appropriate that it should again have been an RAF pilot who was the catalyst for the revival of aerial archaeology in Jordan 70 years later.

Many others people have been important supporters. We are grateful to Alison McQuitty and Patricia Salti who helped launch the enterprise in 1997. Dr Ghazi Bisheh and Dr Fawwaz al-Khraysheh, successive Directors General of the Department of Antiquities who consistently supported our efforts. Two Australian ambassadors — Merry Wickes and John Tilemann have been very supportive. Francesca Radcliffe, whose good company in the field and in the 'backroom', made the thankless task of cataloguing more bearable.

Many others have given advice or responded to queries: John Coles, Samantha Dennis, George Findlater, Bill Finlayson, John Harte, Ina Kehrberg, Bill Lyons, Nofa Nasser, Paul Newson, Alessandra Peruzzetto, Andrew Petersen, Tobias Richter, Charlotte Schriver, Jane Taylor, Alan Walmsley, Alex Wasse, David Wilson. A special thank you to Nadja Qaisi of the CBRL in Amman without whose administrative skills and good humour, no season would have run as smoothly or agreeably.

Several friends and colleagues responded promptly to requests to read parts of the book in draft and we are extremely grateful to: Piotr Bienkowski, Andrew Petersen, Phil Freeman, Kay Prag, Denys Pringle and Alan Walmsley. They are, of course, not responsible for the results.

In 2000 we were flown in an Islander aircraft owned by The Royal Parachute and Aerosports Club of Jordan. We are grateful to Samih Janakat and his son Nart. In 2001 we transferred to Cessna 152s of Sun Aviation, which arranged for one of the authors (RHB) to obtain a Jordanian Private Pilot's Licence. We are delighted to record our thanks to Munqeth R. Mahyar, Captain Osama Hyari, Mohammed Shafaqoy, and Yousri Shahaltough, and 'Ahmed the Engineer'.

We can conclude by offering our thanks to the many delightful people with whom we have worked at the Air Lift Wing at RJAF Marka at Amman, the old Ottoman and RAF base from which German and British pilots flew to photograph archaeological sites in the 1910s, 1920s and 1930s: Brigadier General Ziad Hanandeh, Brigadier General Mohammad Zouabi, Brigadier General Talal abu Qamar, Brigadier General Abd el-Haleem K. Mahafthah, Brigadier General Khalil Kurdi, Colonel Sami Hantoush, Lt. Colonel Nasser Othman, Lt. Colonel Ziad Abu-Ain, Lt. Colonel Hussein Obeidat, Lt. Colonel Omar Sadeq Damra, Major Belal Asfour, Major Mohammad al-Eghwari, Major Samir Ayoub, Captain Bassem al-Hilwani, Captain Daher Talafha, Captain Osama, Captain Rousan, Captain Saket and the several co-pilots who have shared the flying. Especially notable amongst the crewmen who looked after us in flight have been Sergeants Feisal and Bassem Khaled al-Maytah and Lt. Ali Mohammed of military security. Outstanding as pilot, collaborator and friend, has been Major Khaled Migdadi who flew the first flight in 1997 and many of the others since.

Funding for our fieldwork, some at very short notice, came from a variety of sources to all of whom we offer our thanks: The British Academy (in particular Peter Brown), The Prehistoric Society (UK), Society of Antiquaries, London, Seven Pillars of Wisdom Trust, The University of Western Australia, Small ARC Grant (UWA), Robert Kiln Trust, Council for British Research in the Levant, Palestine Exploration Fund and Francesca Radcliffe. With enormous generosity, the Royal Jordanian Air Force underwrote much of the actual cost of flying. We are also grateful to those who acted as referees for the many applications for funds, notably Professor John Coles, David R. Wilson and Philip Freeman.

The book was completed in February 2003, but immediately encountered the difficulty of finding a publisher willing to invest in so much high quality colour photography. After various false leads we were fortunate to secure the support of the Council for British Research in the Levant, which agreed to act as publisher and of David Brown of Oxbow, whose superb bookshops for our subject area will be the distributor.

Finally, some personal observations. First, two friends, now dead, played a large part in stimulating our interest in the Near East, the Roman army and Aerial Archaeology. Professor Barri Jones, an enthusiastic and inspiring teacher at the University of Manchester in the 1970s, taught us both as undergraduates at different times and fanned our enthusiasm for aerial archaeology. From Derrick Riley, a pioneer in aerial archaeology whose first article was published in 1942, we learned a great deal about flying and fieldwork while at the University of Sheffield. We both remember him with respect as an aviator and scholar, and affection as a thoroughly decent man. Last and most important, the patience and support from families and especially wives, Julie Kennedy and Jill Bewley, cannot be over emphasized; without them this adventure could not have been achieved.

This book and the flying that underlies it has been 'work'. But how fortunate we have been to have such work! The photographs illustrate magnificently something of what we saw in our flights and as evocative images speak eloquently of the landscape and the past. We have met and worked with dozens of delightful and interesting people; more than that we have been allowed to fly over places and landscapes that often made us smile just because what we could see below us was so wonderful. It *was* work but much more important, it was fun and a privilege.

David Kennedy, Kalamunda, Western Australia
Bob Bewley, Ashton Keynes, Wiltshire
March 2004

Biographical Note:

David Kennedy, BA (Manchester), D. Phil (Oxford), FSA, FAHA, is a Professor of Roman Archaeology and History at the University of Western Australia. He is the author of several books including *Rome's Desert Frontier from the Air* (with Derrick Riley) (1990), *The Twin Towns of Zeugma on the Euphrates* (1998) and *The Roman Army in Jordan* (2nd edition, 2004).

Robert Bewley, BA (Manchester), M. Phil, PhD (Cambridge), MIFA, FSA, is Head of Survey for English Heritage. He has published extensively including *Prehistoric and Romano-British Settlement in the Solway Plain, Cumbria* (1994), *Lincolnshire's Archaeology from the Air* (1999) *and Prehistoric Settlements* (2nd edition, 2003).

GLOSSARY AND A NOTE ON PLACE-NAMES

Term (plus common alternatives)	Abbreviation	Meaning
'Ain (Ayn, 'ayn)		spring
Bir (bi'r)		well, cistern
Birkeh (Birket)		pool, reservoir
Deir (Dayr)		monastery, shrine
Ghadir		water hole, water hole in wadi
Ghor		lowland, plain depression, marshy plain
Hammam		baths
Husn		fortress
Jebel (Jabal)	J.	mountain, hill
Khan		inn, caravanserai
Khirbet (Khirbat)	Kh.	ruins, village
Muhattat (Mahattat)		station, railroad station
Naqb		pass
Qa'		mudflat
Qal'at		fort
Qasr	Q.	castle, palace, fort
Qaryat		settlement, village
Ras (ra's)		peak, point, mountain
Rujm		cairn, hill, tomb
Siq		narrow pass
Tell (Tall)	T.	hill
Wadi	W.	wadi, stream (usually only seasonal)

Transliteration of place-names from Arabic into the Roman alphabet is notoriously inconsistent and users of this book are likely to find spellings employed here, at variance with those found in other books and on maps. We have normally given preference to the form used by the scholars most involved in writing about specific places, and tried then to be consistent in our usage of common place-name elements, preferring Ain to Ayn and Qasr to Kasr, etc. We have not generally used diacritical marks at all.

CHRONOLOGY AND RULERS

A full chronology of the various dynasties to have ruled over Jordan would be both lengthy and unnecessary. The following is intended to be a helpful guide to the chronologies, dating systems and dynasties, which were of most importance. Those such as the Nabataeans, who ruled directly over the region, are set out in full, while others, for whom Jordan was no more than a part of their domain, are set out more selectively. Because literary sources, coins and inscriptions naming Roman emperors are so abundant and useful as a guide to dating they have been given in full. Likewise the Umayyad dynasty ruling from nearby in Damascus, and the Crusader kings ruling from Jerusalem, are set out in full.

A. Chronology

Although the Palaeolithic begins as much as 2.5 million years ago in Africa, in Jordan the earliest evidence is only about half a million years ago. It extends then for well over 400,000 years. Consequently, all subsequent periods are compressed into the 12,000+ years since then.

In geological chronology, human history is spread across three time periods: Pliocene, Pleistocene and Holocene. The Palaeolithic begins towards the end of the Pliocene, but otherwise coincides with the Pleistocene. The close of the Palaeolithic coincides with the end of the Pleistocene and the beginning of the Holocene *c.* 10,000 before present (bp), the current geological period.

The latter part of the Pleistocene was marked by the advance and retreat of glaciers in the northern hemisphere. While these did not affect the Middle East directly, they did bring about long-term shifts in climate and environment indirectly, with consequences for both human populations and other species. This partly explains why so many of the key sites for the Palaeolithic in Jordan lie today in areas of great aridity — for long periods of the Pleistocene they were far wetter and enjoyed a Mediterranean type of vegetation, now found only much further west and north. The Holocene brought wetter conditions and a spread of forests: it is against this background that the Neolithic period and the beginnings of farming are placed. Each of the main periods is subdivided in various ways by terms (Lower, Middle, etc) letters (A, B, etc) or Roman numerals (I, II, etc).

Dates in prehistory, and to a large extent in history too, are imprecise. Various scientific techniques provide absolute dates, but these are often very broad; more commonly, dating is provided by artefacts, initially distinctive flint tools and then, from the later Neolithic, pottery types and forms. In the historic period written sources become available — not least the Hebrew Bible — but remain relatively rare for some centuries. By the Roman period we often have a wide range and far more abundant dating material, some of which can be very precise — coins, of course, but more precise still, inscriptions and a growing corpus of papyri. The range of sources for dating remains wide thereafter, but the quantities are often much less than in the rich Roman period. On the other hand, with the Ottoman period we start to get access to archival material and with the 19th and 20th centuries it becomes voluminous.

There is considerable variation in the terms employed and even in the meaning given to some of them. Throughout this book, in conformity with most British practice, the term 'Roman' is employed to cover the entire span from the arrival of Pompey the Great, in Syria in 63 BC, to the Battle of the Yarmuk in AD 636 and the end of Roman rule in the region. Readers turning elsewhere should be aware that American, and some other scholars, commonly apply the term 'Byzantine' to the latter half of what we are calling the Roman period, usually beginning with the Christian Empire in AD 324 or even Diocletian in AD 284. There is a common practice too, of treating the last phase of Nabataean independence as 'Nabataean/ Early Roman'.

Readers may find the following tabulation (adapted and expanded from Miller 1991: 27) convenient.

B. Chronological Labels and Dates

Palaeo	**PALAEOLITHIC**	**Before 450,000 – 10,300 bp**
	Lower (Acheulian)	before 450,000 – 150,000 bp
	Middle	150,000 – 45,000 bp
	Upper	45,000 – 20,000/ 16,000 bp
	Epipalaeolithic	20,000 – 10,300 bp

Neo	**NEOLITHIC**	**10300 bp – 5700 BC**
PPNA	Pre-Pottery Neolithic A	10300 – 9600 bp
Early PPNB	Early Pre-Pottery Neolithic B	9600 – 9200 bp
Middle PPNB	Middle Pre-Pottery Neolithic B	9200 – 8500 bp
Late PPNB	Late Pre-Pottery Neolithic B	8500 – 8000 bp
PPNC	Pre-Pottery Neolithic C	8000 – 7500 bp
PN	Pottery Neolithic	7500 – 5700 BC
Chalco	**CHALCOLITHIC**	**5700 – 3600 BC**
EB	**EARLY BRONZE AGE**	**3600 – 2300**
EB I	Early Bronze	3600 – 3100
EB II		3100 – 2750
EB III		2750 – 2300
EB IV		2300 – 2000
MB	**MIDDLE BRONZE AGE**	**2000 – 1500**
MB I		2000 – 1650
MB II		1650 – 1500
LB	**LATE BRONZE AGE**	**1500 – 1200**
LB I		1500 – 1400
LB II		1400 – 1200
IR	**IRON AGE**	**1200 – 300**
IR I		1200 – 900
IR II		900 – 332
Pers(ian) [= IR IIC]		540 – 332
Hell	**HELLENISTIC**	**332 – 64**
Nab	**NABATAEAN**	**300 BC – AD 106**
Rom	**ROMAN**	**64 BC – AD 324**
ERom		64 BC – AD 135
LRom		AD 135 – AD 324
Byz	**BYZANTINE**	**324 – 640**
EByz		324 – 491
LByz		491 – 640
EIsl	**EARLY ISLAMIC**	**640 – 1174**
Um	Umayyad	640 – 750
Abb	Abbasid	750 – 969
Fat	Fatimid	969 – 1071
	Seljuk-Zenjid	1071 – 1174
Crus	**CRUSADER**	**1099 – 1291**
	Early Crusader	1099 – 1187
	Late Crusader	1187 – 1291
LIsl	**LATE ISLAMIC**	**1174 – 1918**
Ay	Ayyubid	1174 – 1263
Mam	Mamluk	1263 – 1516
EOtt	Early Ottoman	1516 – 1703
LOtt	Late Ottoman	1703 – 1918
Mod	**MODERN**	**1918–**
	British Mandate	
	Hashemite	

C. Nabataean King List

The earliest Nabataean rulers known are attested only once each. The first named is an 'Aretas' *c.* 168 BC who is assigned the numeral I with the subsequent rulers following from there. The list only becomes secure with the man we call Obodas III.[1]

Aretas I	*c.* 168 BC
Aretas II	*c.* 120/110 – 96
Obodas I	96 – 85
Rabbel I	85/84
Aretas III	84 – 62/61
Obodas II	62/61 – 59
Malichus I	59 – 30
Obodas III	30 – 9
Aretas IV	9 BC – AD 40
Malichus II	40 – 70
Rabbel II	70 – 106

D. Hellenistic (a selection of the more significant rulers)

Alexander the Great	336 – 323 BC
Syria:	
Seleucus I Nicator	321 – 281 BC
Antiochus I	281 – 261
Antiochus III 'the Great'	223 – 187
Antiochus IV Epiphanes	175 – 164
Egypt:	
Ptolemy I Soter	323 – 282 BC
Cleopatra VII	69 – 30
Judaea:	
Herod the Great	40 – 4 BC

E. Eras

From the Hellenistic period onwards several 'eras' were employed in the region and dates can be found expressed in terms of all of them though principally the first and last:

Seleucid	dated from 312/11 BC
Pompeian	dated from 62 BC
Gabinian	dated from 55 BC
Era of the Province of Arabia	dated from AD 106

E.g. Year 42 of the Era of Arabia is AD 147/8 (because the era did not begin on the 1st January but during the year).

F. Roman Emperors

Augustus			30BC – AD14
Tiberius	)		14 – 37
Gaius (Caligula)	)	Julio-Claudian dynasty	37 – 41
Claudius	)		41 – 54
Nero	)		54 – 68
Galba			68 – 69
Otho			69
Vitellius			69
Vespasian	)		69 – 79
Titus	)	Flavian dynasty	79 – 81
Domitian	)		81 – 96
Nerva			96 – 98
Trajan			98 – 117
Hadrian			117 – 138
Antoninus Pius	)		138 – 161
Marcus Aurelius	)		
(& LuciusVerus)	)		161 – 169

[1] From Nehmé and Villeneuve 1999: 148.

FURTHER READING

A detailed bibliography can be found on the web at:

http://www.classics.uwa.edu.au/projects/AJAbibliography

Rollin, S. and Streetly, J. (2002) *Blue Guide Jordan,* 3rd ed., London

Meyers, E.M. (ed.) *The Oxford Encyclopedia of Archaeology in the Near East,* New York, 1997 (5 volumes).
This contains numerous articles, some very good but uneven overall, relating to specific events, periods and places.

MacDonald, B., Adams, R. and Bienkowski, P. (eds) (2001) *The Archaeology of Jordan,* Sheffield
A very useful collection of substantial essays on each of the main periods plus others on specific themes. It also has an up-to-date bibliography.

Finally, a book intended for a wider audience:
Bienkowski, P. (1991) *Treasures from an Ancient Land. The Art of Jordan,* Stroud

LIST OF ILLUSTRATIONS

(Film references for individual photographs are in brackets with the date of photography.)

7. INTO HISTORY: MOABITES ETC

8. THE NABATAEANS

9. GREEKS AND ROMANS

10. THE ROMAN ARMY

11. CHRISTIAN ROMAN JORDAN

14. THE OTTOMAN AND BRITISH EMPIRES

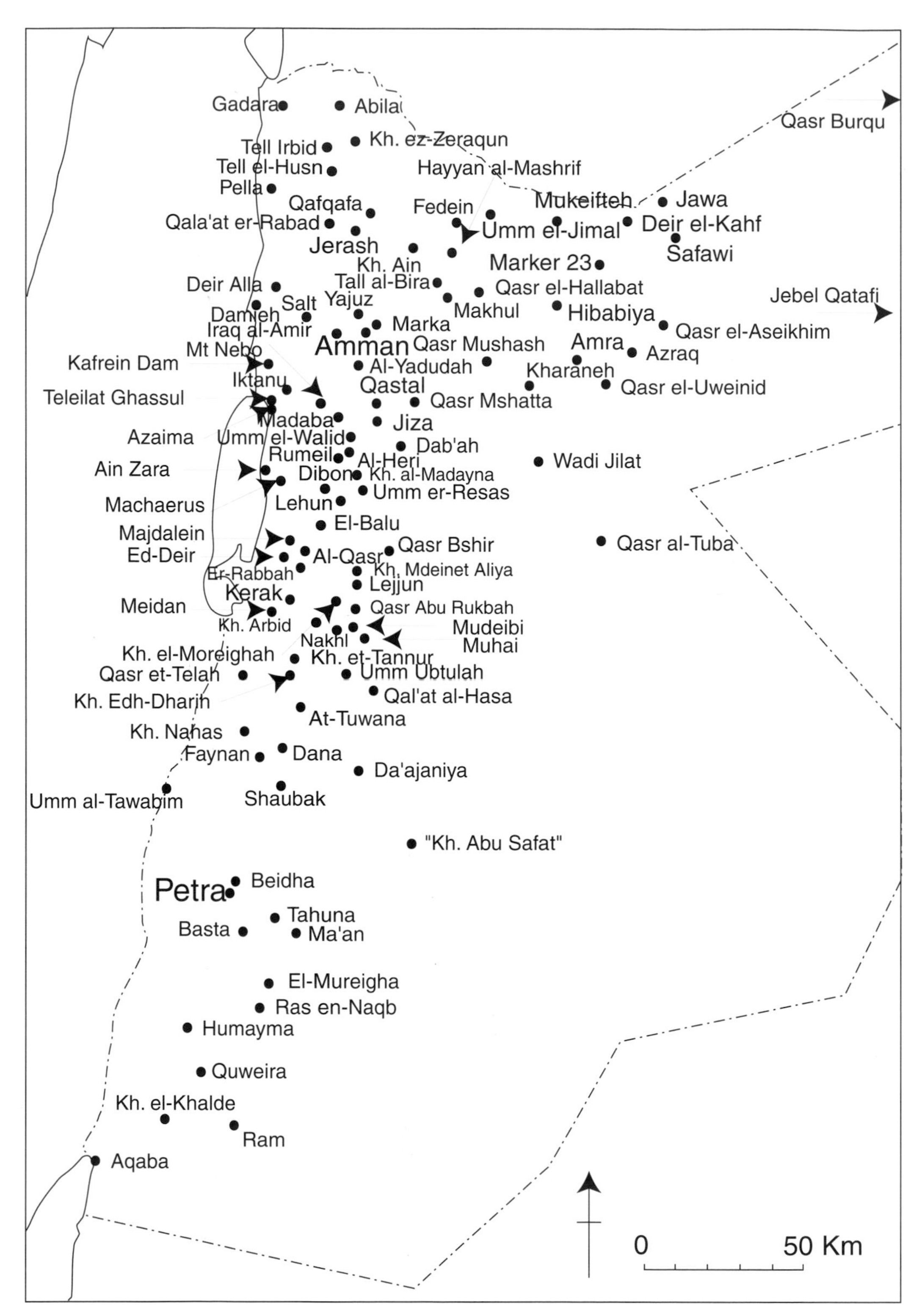

Fig. 1.1: Map of Jordan showing the principal places mentioned in this volume

1. INTRODUCTION

JORDAN is part of the Holy Land, that small but remarkable corner of the Mediterranean lands, from which the three great monotheistic religions of the world sprang. Places currently situated in Jordan figure prominently in the Old and New Testaments, in Talmudic texts and in the Qoran. Names many of us, whether religious not, will be familiar with belong here — Moab, Midianites, Ammon, the Decapolis, Machaerus and many more.

Jordan is part too, of what used to be called the Fertile Crescent, the region stretching in an arc from the head of the Persian Gulf, through Mesopotamia, down the coast of the Levant to the Nile Valley. It was here, that many of the seminal developments in the history of the modern human species, first appeared — the domestication of crops and animals, the beginnings of urbanism and the emergence of some of the first state societies and first empires. Many of the fundamental elements of life in today's world society can be traced to origins in this region — e.g. farming, writing, and urban living.

Jordan played an important part in this development — but more as a place of transition (as it is today) rather than the scene of the major developments themselves. Much of modern Jordan is steppe or desert, what the Bible calls 'wilderness'; it was *from* Jordan (traditionally Mt Nebo, cf. Fig. 11.1) that Moses was shown Canaan, the 'land of milk and honey'. But the area covered by Jordan was frequently part of a bigger world. Some of the major sites of early Near Eastern prehistory are found there — the 8,000 year-old Neolithic site of Beidha, near Petra, is the obvious instance (Fig. 5.1), and the Bronze Age city at Jawa, in the black basalt desert. To later periods belong some of the more important examples of their respective periods: the still amazing Nabataean city of Petra in its mountain valley (Fig. 8.1); the Roman city of Gerasa (Jarash) (Fig. 9.4); the remarkable Islamic 'desert castle' of Qasr Mshatta (Fig. 12.1); Kerak represents one of the most magnificent examples of a Crusader castle (Fig. 13.1); and, if the Ottoman period seems impoverished by comparison, we should not overlook the well-preserved example of an early modern fort like Qal'at el-Hasa (Fig. 14.3), situated along the Pilgrim Road which devout Muslims followed up and down the length of Jordan on their way to and from Mecca.

The modern state of Jordan contains limited natural resources, but these have been fully exploited and the land most extensively and intensively developed when it belonged to one of the major players of the wider world. The great empires of the Near East and Egypt, the profound cultural pulses of Hellenistic Egypt and Syria, the centuries as part of the Roman Empire, succeeded by an Islamic empire ruled from the Umayyad capital of Damascus, or later from the more distant centres of the Abbasid, Fatimid, Ayyubid, Mamluk and Ottoman empires, have all needed this region's resources to further their imperial desires. Indeed, one might also include the final empire, the British, to which Jordan belonged for a generation in the 20th century. Arguably Jordan — or perhaps its components — is an example of one of those Mediterranean micro-regions which flourish most when integrated with a wider world.

The sites mentioned so far will probably be familiar to many readers; or some of them will. This brings us to one of the justifications for our book, to highlight the rich archaeological heritage of Jordan. The list above, though short, may well be all that even the better-informed tourist will know of the archaeological heritage of Jordan. Petra is an exception; it is rightly a place of World Heritage Site status and significance, and often the sole reason for a visit to Jordan. However, the Graeco-Roman city at Jarash is a simple excursion from Amman and some visitors will take the opportunity of a journey to Petra to include the superb castle of Kerak. Those with a religious interest will make an excursion to Madaba and Mt Nebo, to view its churches, mosaics ... and see the Promised Land. A few hardier souls may take in at least the more accessible of the Desert Castles — Qasr el-Kharaneh, Qusayr Amra and perhaps Qasr el-Azraq. These are superb places and often stunningly well-preserved, but they are still only a small part of what Jordanian archaeology has to offer.

A primary objective of this book is to stress and illustrate the immense richness of Jordan's cultural heritage and encourage tourism beyond the handful of well-known archaeological sites. Petra is unique and Kerak is a prime example of a Crusader castle. But there is much more. The Nabataeans also created the great temple of Khirbat et-Tannur and the remote sanctuary at Ramm (Fig. 8.4). The student of medieval castles can also take in Qala'at er-Rabad (Fig. 13.4) built on its eminence, as a defence *against* the Crusaders and commanding a valley leading to the Jordan Valley; Shaubak castle in the south (Fig. 13.2); Wu'eira castle (Fig. 13.3) on the cliffs beside Petra; and Jazirat al-Faroun, on its island in the Gulf of Aqaba. The

Fig. 1.2: The authors and crew at RJAF Marka: Bewley, Kennedy, Major Khaled Migdadi, Lt. Ali Mohammad, Crewman. Note the wide door of the Huey in the background, providing almost uninterrupted vision (APA02/CP20.20A (RHB), 2 October 2002)

Romanist has an embarrassment of choice. For those interested in cities there is not just Jarash (Fig. 9.4) and Amman (Fig. 9.3), but Pella (Fig. 9.5), Gadara (Fig. 9.6), Capitolias and Abila (Fig. 11.2), with circuses, a dozen theatres, baths, and hundreds of metres of colonnaded streets between them. Beyond these are smaller towns at Umm el-Jimal (Fig. 11.3), Yajuz (Fig. 11.5), Sadaqa and a dozen other important ruins. Early Christian churches, many with stunning mosaic pavements, are everywhere — 15 at Jarash alone, another 15 in the small town of Umm el-Jimal, while the concentration at Madaba provides a delightful day out to its Archaeological Park. Roman military interest is catered for by some of the best-preserved forts of the entire Roman Empire — Qasr Bshir (Fig. 10.6), Da'ajaniya (Fig. 10.7), Deir el-Kahf all have walls standing several metres high; Qasr el-Aseikhim (Fig. 10.8), on its conical hill, is surely one of the most evocative desert forts anywhere; Lejjun (Fig. 10.5), whose very name (Legion) preserves its origin, offers 4.6 ha/ 11.5 acres of fortress within an easy drive of Amman; and there are, literally, dozens more such places. Roman roads are everywhere and one can still walk alongside stretches of the great *Via Nova Traiana* (Fig. 9.10) and see milestones lying where they fell, some recording its extent, 'from the boundaries of Syria as far as the Red Sea' — a mere 350 km.

Prehistory and the early historic period provide abundant sites of all kinds, from prehistoric hunting grounds (see the section on 'kite' sites and Fig. 5.4), villages like Basta and Beidha (Figs 5.1–5.2), through great tells in the Jordan Valley recalling Bronze Age urbanization, thousands of dolmens scattered over hillsides, Moabite hill forts (Figs 7.5–7.7) and the thousands of remains in the deserts beyond. Likewise, the Islamic centuries offer the converted Roman fort of Qasr el-Hallabat (Fig. 10.4) with its 'early mosque, scattered houses and irrigated garden', lavish residences at Qastal (Fig. 12.6), Qasr Mushash (Fig. 12.2), Umm el-Walid (Fig. 12.7) and the small town at Aqaba (Fig. 12.8).

The 19th and 20th centuries offer a string of Hajj castles at regular intervals along the Desert Highway, from Syria to the Hejaz and beyond (Figs 14.1–14.3); the Hejaz Railway itself is an artefact of the opening up of this region in modern times (Fig. 14.6); the trenches of the Ottoman Army can still be traced from the campaigns of 1917–18 (Fig. 14.7A); the Germans built, not just the railway, but in 1917–18 the forerunners of the current airfields at Marka (Amman) and where the Queen Alia International Airport lies today (Fig. 14.8A). Another imperial power, Britain, created forts like those at Azraq Shishan and Quweira (Fig. 14.7B) for detachments of the Arab Legion, that brought peace and stability to the bulk of the country, which lay beyond the settled heartlands of the northwest. We should not forget the battle fought as recently as 1922 when aircraft and armoured cars turned back a raid by *c.* 4,000 tribesmen at Umm el-Amad, a few kilometres northwest of the current international airport at Amman. The corollary to the great antiquity of much of what Jordan has to offer is that the country itself is so new. Outstanding amongst the new is the great Hashemite Friday Mosque in Amman. Striking residences are springing up in the countryside all around Amman, which, to paraphrase the former French President, Clemenceau (when viewing the recently completed New Delhi), will make magnificent ruins for the future!

This is still only the tiny tip of an iceberg. In 1994, the Department of Antiquities of Jordan published a database of known archaeological sites, which ran to some 8,000 items. Hundreds more have been added since then by ground surveys. More than that still, the interpretation of aerial photographs taken in 1953 over western Jordan identified some 25,000 'sites'. That too, is only part of the reality. Jordan has an enormously rich and varied archaeological resource, with probably over 100,000 sites of every period, shape and size in an area of 89,000 sq km.

In developed countries archaeology is a significant economic factor. Archaeological investigation might be viewed as expensive, or a hindrance to development, but it can also be seen as an investment. Societies have an obligation to record and, as far as possible, protect the cultural heritage within their borders. Ultimately it belongs to us all — the destruction of the Buddhas of Bamian brought powerful international condemnation. International resources have been mustered with increasing frequency, to salvage important remains (the Egyptian temple at Abu Simbel springs to mind), to press for access (the front page report and editorial of the New York Times concerning Zeugma in Turkey) and to try and halt future damage or erosion. This is partly in response to the public's wish to have these sites preserved. But it also pays. Any visitor to Britain, France or the United States will be impressed by the way in which thousands of archaeological sites are managed, provide employment and income. A recent survey in England showed that of the 19.3 million overseas 'visits', 37% were to heritage sites, which generated 3.5 billion pounds.

More than mere economics, the promotion of cultural heritage is a branch of international diplomacy. The presentation and dissemination of information, with regard to what a country has to offer, is an advertisement for that country and helps mould external perceptions. It is a part of the creation of what is today called 'soft power', cultural influence. Petra, Qasr Mshatta, Qusayr Amra and Qala'at er-Rabad, for example, are powerful and evocative reminders of the achievements of Arab and Muslim culture in a world in which, all too often, their present descendants are viewed negatively.

The photographs presented in this book illustrate these achievements in a unique way, and were taken as part of a series of seasons of flying for archaeology (Chapter 4). Aerial reconnaissance is possibly the most powerful tool for finding sites and is invaluable for helping to understand them. The longer-term objective is to have a routine programme of aerial reconnaissance to find, map, interpret and monitor sites of all kinds, just as is the case in developed countries. Jordan is virtually unique outside the developed world in allowing such work and it should be a model for others of what *can* be achieved and *should* be done.

Sites were selected and photographs taken with the idea in mind of a book of air photographs modelled on that by Raymond Schoder, *Ancient Greece from the Air* (*Wings Over Hellas* in the US edition). Schoder brilliantly evoked the richness and quality of the archaeology of Classical Greece in a series of colour air photographs. We hope this book will go further in bringing the superb archaeological remains of all periods of Jordan into the living rooms of those interested in the past and encouraging tourists in Jordan to go beyond the beaten track.

This is not a guidebook, but it may be treated as a guide to some of the most significant sites of Jordan. Inevitably the selection is a very personal one and we have concentrated on those with major remains. The problem was not in finding a hundred or more such places, but in keeping the list below 500. Although few places in Jordan remain truly remote and surfaced roads are everywhere, some places are hard to find without a guide. Even from the air, we often needed an old vertical air photograph in hand to guide us to the places we wanted to see and photograph. Conversely, most places illustrated here can be found easily, or with a little effort.

The management and promotion of cultural heritage in Jordan has changed a great deal in recent years. In the early 1970s few archaeological sites were managed and even Petra could be accessed simply and at a minimal fee. Today Petra is a major tourist destination and a dozen other places — Gadara, Gerasa, Qusayr Amra, Qasr el-Kharaneh, Qala'at er-Rabad, Madaba, Mt Nebo, Kerak ... are being actively marketed. The Department of Antiquities has long played a key role in protecting and revealing the archaeology of Jordan and has been assisted by various foreign 'schools' and institutes operating in Jordan. The recent establishment of the Jordan Tourist Board has seen a further important development, with a spate of attractive and professional pieces of literature. Peace and development can only accelerate the process. It is an exciting prospect and an important one. But it also brings dangers, which the Department of Antiquities will find increasingly demanding.

Development poses a threat to cultural heritage, and it is easy and understandable for economics to be more prominent than archaeology. But the temptation must be resisted. Not only is the past of long-term cultural importance, it also has the potential to assist in the future economic stability of any region. Everywhere in the world cultural heritage faces threats. Jordan is no different and in the work that follows the viewer will encounter numerous examples (see especially Ma'an, Figs 4.11 and 14.9A).

The structure of this book is simple. This chapter is followed by three brief chapters sketching the geography and environment, and how it has changed through history (Ch. 2); an outline of the history from earliest times to the present day (Ch. 3); and a survey of how aerial archaeology is done and why (Ch. 4). The core of the book is Chapters 5–14. These trace and illustrate the archaeology through aerial images. The material is arranged chronologically from prehistory onwards. Some periods are especially rich and have been divided so that chapters are roughly the same length but may deal with periods of variable length. The immensely rich Roman period is the obvious example for reasons explained more fully in Chapter 3.

Within each chapter there is a selection of sites, drawn from as wide an area of Jordan as possible. Each chapter is introduced by a brief outline of the period cross-referenced to the examples that follow and other relevant sites elsewhere in the book. In most cases a panoramic image introduces the site and its context; a second image looks more closely at the site or some part of it. A few major sites — Petra and Jarash — merit more extensive treatment; some pairings are of different sites but related by a common theme.

2. THE LAND AND ITS PEOPLE

It has been a great privilege to fly over Jordan's wide variety of landscapes and environments. Within a short time one is transported from one distinctive area to another and sees the equally varied types of archaeological site — a reflection of the different responses to the exploitation of the natural environment from 10,000 BC to the present day. The reader of this book, browsing through the scores of images, will, vicariously, experience Jordan's archaeological sites and their multitudinous contexts. Hence, a short chapter defining and describing the physical background will provide some understanding of the archaeology: the overall pattern of sites, their specific locations, the types and forms and the differential preservation.

The Land

Jordan is a small country: it is some 460 km north to south by 355 km in width, a total of about 92,000 sq km **(Fig. 2.1).** Put in context, the United Kingdom is 244,110 sq km, California 411,049, New South Wales 801,428 and Japan 377,835. There are 6 major landscape zones, easily noticeable as you travel from one area to another. These are: the broad Jordan Valley; the Highlands of Ajlun in the northwest; the high plateaux running along the west side overlooking the Rift Valley as far south as the Shera'a Mountains; the band of steppe, or pre-desert, running east of and parallel to this western strip; (the two great oases at Azraq and al-Jafr and the broad trough of the Wadi Sirhan) the Hisma Desert in the south; and finally, the great sweep of deserts of various types, from the sandy Hisma northeastwards, through a chert desert, to the black Basalt Desert from Azraq out into the panhandle towards the Iraqi frontier. Most of Jordan is desert, arid and unproductive.

Jordan's borders are relatively recent and largely artificial creations. In the early 1920s, the League of Nations divided up the former Turkish possessions in the Near East into a group of 'mandates' for administration by Britain and France. Frontiers were established dividing what was then called Transjordan from its newly defined neighbours: Palestine, Syria, Iraq, and Saudi Arabia. Only on the west is the country's frontier sharply defined by nature. There the political border with Israel and Palestine is the north–south line of the Rift Valley — the River Jordan, the Dead Sea and then the dry trough of the Wadi Araba, which merges into the Gulf of Aqaba. All of it is below sea level, reaching as much as minus 406 m at the Dead Sea, the lowest point on earth. Elsewhere the borders are largely artificial creations, marked by the long straight lines characteristic of the bold imperial planners of the colonial powers of a century ago. In the north the frontier with Syria begins with the natural slash of the deep Wadi Yarmuk and continues in a meandering line for a time, along the fringe of what, at that time, was the 'frontier of settlement' in southern Syria, the Hauran. But then it continues as a series of straight lines striking off northeast across the forbidding Basalt Desert. The eastern frontier with Iraq and the eastern and southern with Saudi Arabia are the same — a series of long straight lines in the desert which give Jordan its distinctive outline, including the broad 'pan-handle' corridor linking it to Iraq. Since the initial layout there have been some adjustments, especially in relation to Saudi Arabia.

Inevitably these frontiers slice artificially through landscapes and environments. In the north, east and south in particular, they cut across the transhumance routes of nomads who have traversed these regions annually for millennia. Only in the south, on the narrow 26 km frontage on the Gulf of Aqaba, does Jordan have an outlet to the sea and to the world's oceans.

Most visitors to Jordan — especially if arriving by air and from the west — will firstly appreciate the Jordan Valley, a wildly meandering stream, in the midst of a broad band of highly intensive cultivation on both Israeli and Jordanian banks. Next, the aircraft will cross the range of limestone hills of the northwest. Amman itself is on the southeastern fringe where they are highest at *c.* 800 m. They extend northwestwards with spot heights of *c.* 500 m at Jarash, *c.* 300 m at Umm Qeis overlooking the Golan Heights and Lake Tiberias, and over 1,100 m around Ajlun to the west of Jarash **(Fig. 2.2)**. These hills, the Highlands of Ajlun, form an important element in the landscape, rising up on the east side of the Jordan Valley through a vertical distance of more than 1,500 m.

South of these highlands, the land gives way to a long upland plateau, divided into three by the Wadi Mujib and the Wadi el Hasa. The first part was what was once called Moab, and the third, ancient Edom. The hills rise again much further south as the pink sandstone hills, the Jebal Shera'a, in which the most famous of all Jordan's archaeological sites, Petra, is situated. It is in the similar red sandstone hills further southeast at Jebal Ram, that the highest peak in Jordan is found (1,734 m).

Highlands, plateau and hills again are all marked by a series of valleys running westwards down into the Rift

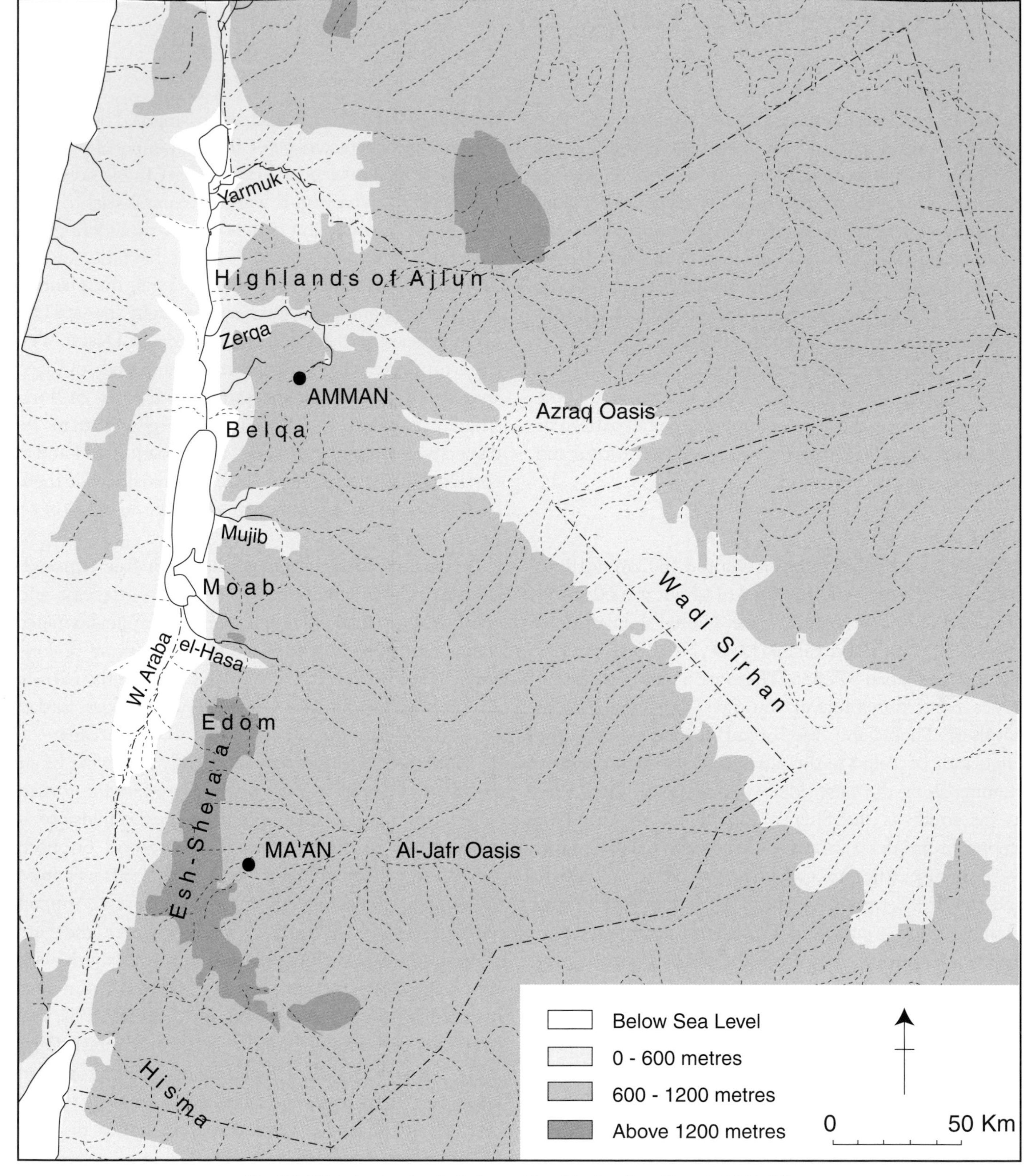

Fig. 2.1: Map showing the physical geography of Jordan (from Kennedy 2004: 30)

Valley. Some are major cuts in the landscape and contain significant streams. In the north, the border with Syria is the formidable Wadi Yarmuk, a major perennial watercourse, just south of Lake Tiberias (formerly the Sea of Galilee). A fertile tributary of this is the Wadi Shallalah, a barrier to movement (Fig. 6.4) but which contains a number of important prehistoric tell sites and a rare example of a Roman bridge (Fig. 9.10B). Next comes the Wadi Zarqa **(Fig. 2.9)**, the most important perennial watercourse in Jordan after the River Jordan and ahead of the Yarmuk. It rises near Amman and even today is a perennial stream from there to the Jordan. Next comes the Wadi Wala, a major gash on the landscape but dwarfed by the greatest of them all, the Wadi Mujib (the Biblical Arnon) **(Fig. 2.3)** and even the Wadi al-Hasa furthest south (Figs 6.7A, 8.3A and 14.3A). The force of nature is clearly visible as these wadis widen with depth, and disgorge into the Rift Valley.

Fig. 2.2: The Highlands of Ajlun (APA98/ SL23.27, 16 May 1998)

In places, these sub-regions shade off into one another; sometimes they are marked by major natural breaks, which influenced communications and the patterns of human settlement, and created the immensely varied landscape with the strikingly different environments one sees still. The highlands around Jarash and Ajlun are a delight throughout the year. The immense trough created by the Wadi Mujib and its tributaries is an arresting sight, but it and other great wadis are also influential as physical barriers to communication and to political unity. About 25 km south of Kerak lies the Wadi el-Hasa. Although less imposing than the Wadi Mujib it is still a great landmark, running some 50 km from the steppe westwards and down into the Dead Sea. In the late 3rd century AD when the Roman province of Arabia was divided the break, quite naturally, came here, cutting off Moab in the north, from the heartland of the old Nabataean kingdom south of the Hasa and the Hisma Desert below that **(Fig. 2.4).** The deserts dominate the landscape — the Black Basalt Desert covers much of the country north and east of the Azraq Oasis. Despite its forbidding appearance (cf. Figs 5.4–5.6), it supports some vegetation and the runoff from the higher ground in southern Syria, can be trapped to water animals and people. In contrast, the chert desert to the south, then the badlands **(Fig. 2.5**) and sand desert further south still are often bleak places. The landscape of the Wadi Ram is arresting but still profoundly inhospitable **(Fig. 2.6).**

A key map of Jordan is one that defines the soils **(Fig. 2.7).** Once again, it is to the northwest one turns for the richest soils; the rich *terra rosas*, usually forming on limestone, with a 50% clay content so they hold moisture well, but which are susceptible to erosion, as they are not free draining. Combined with high rainfall, the rich soils of the Highlands of Ajlun represent one of the major agricultural areas of Jordan. Stretching south is another group of lesser, but still fertile soils dominating the western plateau (cf. Fig. 13.8). Next come the rich soils of the Jordan Valley **(Fig. 2.8)**, amenable to irrigation and turning the narrow strip into a market garden for intensive cultivation. Finally, the steppe lands east and southeast of Amman have fertile soils, but are dependent on limited rainfall and only truly open to intensive settlement with all the sustained effort

Fig. 2.4: The Hisma Desert (APA98/ SL41.34, 20 May 1998)

the region requires when there is enduring peace and security (cf. Fig. 14.2).

In total these arable soils represent only 2.87% of the entire country — cf. Britain: 26.41% USA: 19.32% and Australia: 6.88% — and explain a great deal about modern Jordan and earlier settlement.

Climate and Rainfall

Jordan is a dry land with water at a premium; today it is hot and dry from May to October, cooler and wetter from November to April. Throughout history, the focus of human activity has been constrained and directed by the location of perennial water courses, springs, oases, and the rainfall pattern. In a cruel twist of fate, the major water concentration in the country is the highly saline and aptly named Dead Sea (cf. Fig. 9.2), the limited settlement around its shores being determined by a handful of local springs.

Early farmers required water for themselves and for their stock and, where agriculture was possible, they needed water for either rainfed agriculture or irrigation farming. The water resources can be swiftly summarized. Along the northwest side runs the River Jordan in its deep valley, at least 200 m below sea level **(Fig. 2.8)**. Today it is a shrunken miserable stream, massive modern extraction having carried off water for people and the intensive market gardening agriculture of the rich soils in the broad valley. In the far northwest the Wadi Yarmuk runs from the east, down into the Jordan Valley, while further south it is paralleled by the Wadi Zarqa (the Biblical Jabbok) **(Fig. 2.9)**, both of them significant perennial rivers before modern extraction upstream. Further south again, there are the streams of the Wadi Mujib **(Fig. 2.3)** and the Wadi el-Hasa (cf. Figs 6.7A and 8.3A) and all along the plateau from the Wadi Yarmuk southwards, there are smaller wadis coming down into the Jordan Valley or the Dead Sea carrying at least seasonal streams. The same wadis are often marked by springs which have attracted settlement throughout history.

The northwestern corner of Jordan has the highest rainfall **(Fig. 2.10)** — averaging over 600 mm in the highlands around Ajlun and still as much as 300 mm around Amman. Inevitably, this relatively well-watered area is one of the most intensively settled today, as it was in earlier periods too.

Water becomes scarcer as one moves south and east. Rainfall declines sharply in this direction although there

Fig. 2.3: The Wadi Mujib (APA03/ SL26.1, 30 September 2004)

Fig. 2.5: 'Badlands' west of the Al-Jafr Oasis (APA98/ SL18.19A, 14 May 1998)

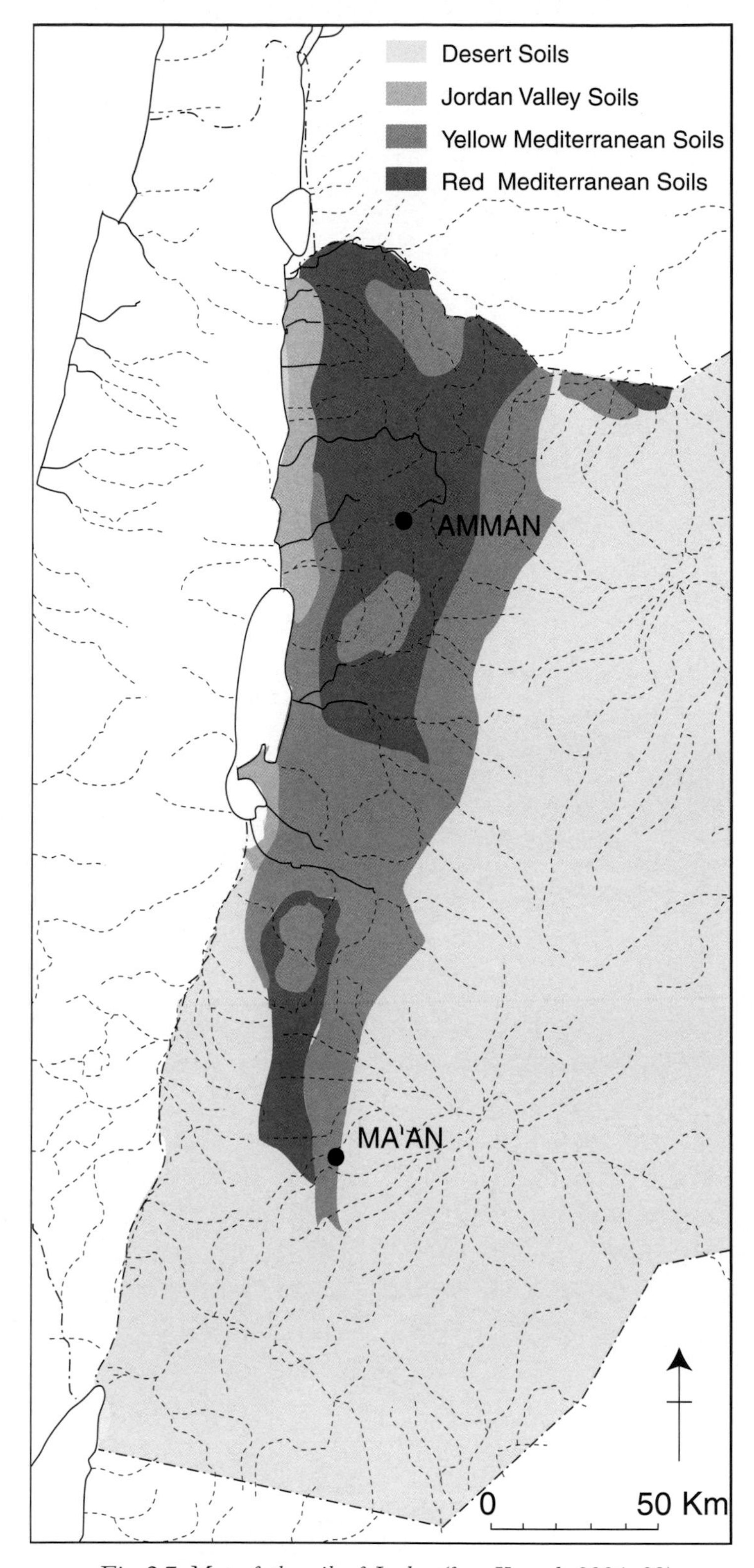

Fig. 2.7: Map of the soils of Jordan (from Kennedy 2004: 32)

are pockets of relatively high (200–300 mm) rainfall on the plateau east of the Dead Sea and in the highlands around Petra, but elsewhere it soon falls to 100 mm or less — half the minimum needed for most rainfed agriculture. The effect on the landscape is easily illustrated when rainfall is seasonal and wadis can be dry for months, even years on end **(Fig. 2.11)** then, briefly, greened by a period of winter rain **(Fig. 2.13).** There are oases — the Al-Jafr Oasis in the southeast and, in particular, the Azraq Oasis in the northeast (cf. Fig. 12.10A). Until it was pumped almost dry in the 1990s, Azraq was a major area of fresh water, with extensive marshlands, and attractive to numerous species of fauna, including migratory birds.

Most of the low-rainfall area has little to offer: not only is water scarce and highly restricted in summer, but soils are poor, restricting the scope even for pasturage for nomads and the hardier domestic species. In such an environment people were inevitably forced into limited areas of better conditions. But they also

Fig. 2.6: The Wadi Ram area (APA98/ SL41.33, 20 May 1998)

responded to the limitations of nature, rising to the challenge by 'harvesting' such rainfall as there was. It was collected in reservoirs and cisterns for people, animals and garden crops, and more generally rainfall from a wide area could be concentrated onto smaller areas for agriculture by clearing obstacles to runoff, creating channels or constructing dams. This adaptation to the challenges of nature began early and became a constant feature of settlement through the ages (cf. Figs 10.4, 12.5A, 12.7C, 12.10B, 14.1B). The technology is often simple; the ingenuity of populations through millennia is on display everywhere in Jordan and is immensely impressive.

In the steppe/ pre-desert there was considerable scope for development. Soils were poorer and rainfall at the margins of what was required. However, given security, people invested the time and effort necessary to harvest water resources and maximize their use. One of the most notable features of this effort is the succession of low parallel walls. They are found built across wadi courses in such areas, creating small fields but also ponding seasonal water flow and trapping soils for modest farming **(Fig. 2.12;** cf. Fig. 4.8).

As we now know, the distant past experienced different climatic patterns and that has to be borne in mind when studying the prehistory of the country. As noted in the chronological discussion, much of prehistory occurred during far wetter conditions. In general there has been no significant change in climate in historic times. The key term, however, is 'significant'. Minor fluctuations in marginal areas can be highly significant for the success of farming and explain the ebb and flow of settlement in the steppe lands in particular. In short, the settlement of marginal lands is certainly affected by security, but we must also consider the influence of minor fluctuations on a fragile system with no scope for spreading risk.

In summary, the Jordan Valley is humid and can be lush with vegetation; the highland zone is cool, well-watered with extensive tree cover and a Mediterranean climate; the plateaux are often treeless but provide good soils; the steppe is open and becoming arid in its feel, but can be intensively settled; the deserts vary from offering pockets of vegetation to forbidding aridity.

Resources

Jordan is not an oil state and natural resources are limited: bitumen on the Dead Sea was being harvested over 2,000 years ago and copper from the mines in the Wadi Araba was being exploited in the Chalcolithic. Agriculture has been important in the areas described above and its products are notable amongst the popular elements in the mosaics of Roman Jordan. But, as we have seen, arable land is scarce — less than 3% of the total.

But Jordan has another resource in its location: it is on a crossroads. Sea traffic on the Red Sea from the Yemen, or further east from India, could terminate where Aqaba now stands (Figs 12.8 and 13.7); coastal traffic through the Hejaz arrived at the same place with the produce of the Yemen; the Wadi Sirhan offered a great natural route linking the Persian Gulf with the Hauran. The routes terminated beyond Jordan in the great urban centres of inland Syria and the Levantine coast or, via the Mediterranean, with the wider world beyond: Egypt, the Aegean and the Western Mediterranean.

Jordan's Mediterranean climate in the more hospitable west supports all the traditional crops, beginning with the so-called 'Mediterranean triad': cereals, grapes and olives. Naturally these are concentrated most intensively in the fertile and well-watered northwest and the plateau to the south, but pockets are found elsewhere, and the Hauran along the border with Syria is especially notable. The archaeological record and depictions in art allow us to add a range of other crops grown in the region, such as peaches, nuts, and figs.

Domesticated animals are, likewise, the expected species found throughout the Mediterranean and Near East, and attested in the archaeological record through their bones: cattle, pigs, sheep and goats, chickens, horses, donkeys, and camels; and other non-food animals such as dogs and cats. Humans could also exploit wild animals: hare are popular inclusions in mosaics of the Roman period, as are gazelle. The latter were still to be found in the tens of thousands into the 20th century and were evidently an important hunted food source in the past (cf. Fig. 5.4). Many other species, now extinct, sometimes only quite recently, are attested: oryx and roe deer; lions (common in Umayyad times but extinct by the 15th century AD), foxes (one was seen from our helicopter at Qasr el-Aseikhim (Fig. 10.8) in 1998), wild cats, cheetahs, leopards and hyenas; crocodiles; ostriches, bustards and falcons. The Azraq Oasis was, until recently, the home of numerous species of birds and, as one of the world's great natural wetlands, visited by huge numbers of migratory birds. An Umayyad building there has yielded numerous relief decorated blocks bearing images of the wildlife the people of that time will have seen.

The people

Jordan has a very small population — in 2003 it was estimated at 5.46 million; most live in the northwestern

Fig. 2.8: The Jordan Valley (APA 98/ SL26.32, 17 May 1998)

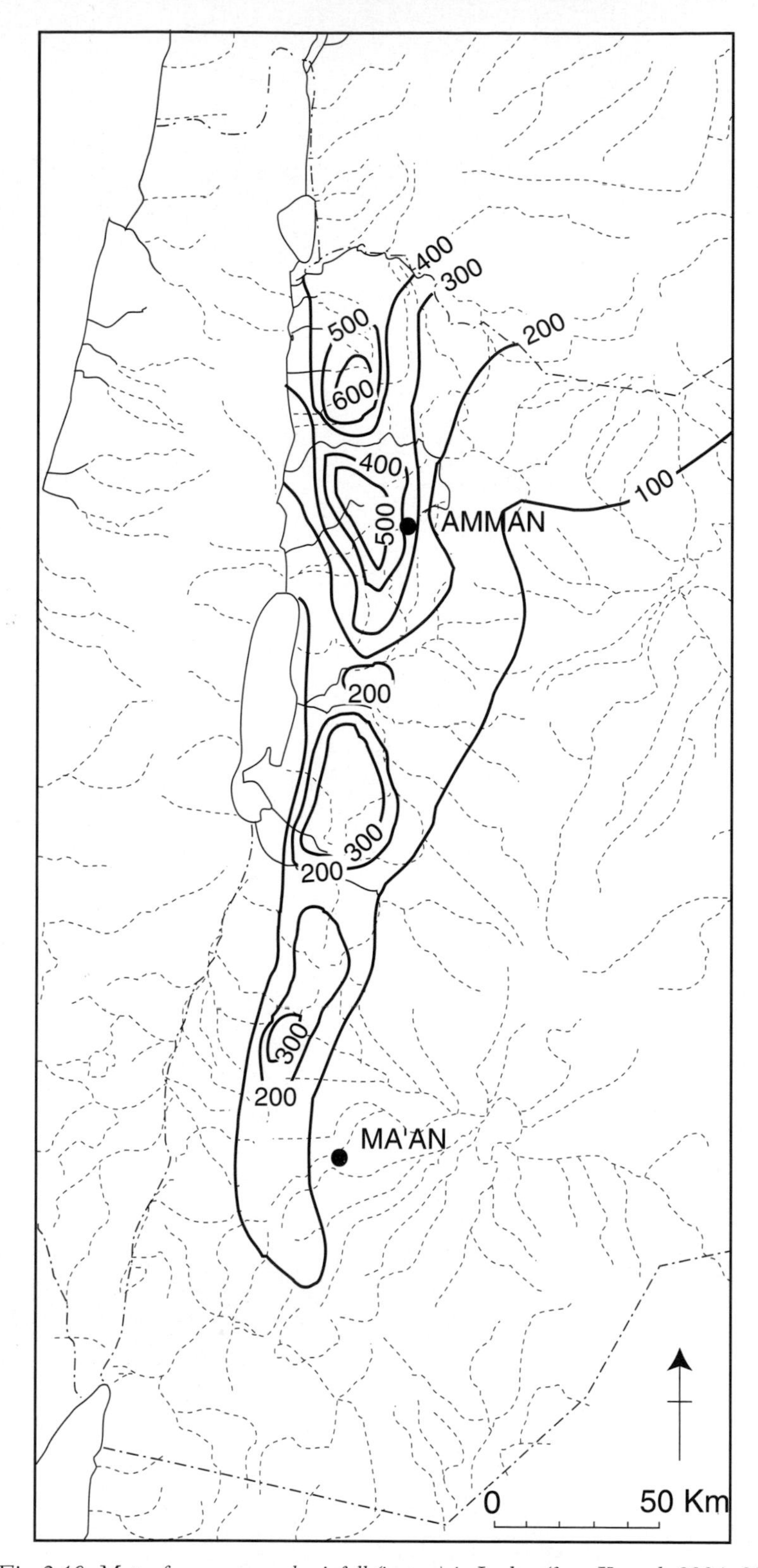

Fig. 2.10: Map of mean annual rainfall (in mm) in Jordan (from Kennedy 2004: 32)

corner, with the capital city, Amman, alone accounting for *c.* 1.9 million. The population is overwhelmingly Sunni Muslim (92%) and predominantly Arab (98%).

In the past the population was likewise overwhelmingly Semitic and Arab, but with a small mix from migration during those periods when Jordan was part of the empires of other people: Israelites, Assyrians, Babylonians, Persians, Greeks, Romans, Ottomans and of course the subject peoples of these empires.

Population sizes are notoriously difficult to estimate. The Bronze Age saw one major growth in population and an even larger one occurred in Roman times. One expert has recently estimated Greater Syria to have had a population in AD 14 of 4.3 million and another suggests 'Western Palestine' (= Israel and Palestine) may have had a maximum of 1 million people in AD 600. The latter is probably far too high and, whatever the true figure, contemporary Jordan will have had far

Fig. 2.9: The Wadi Zarqa (APA99/ SL19.32, 16 June 1999)

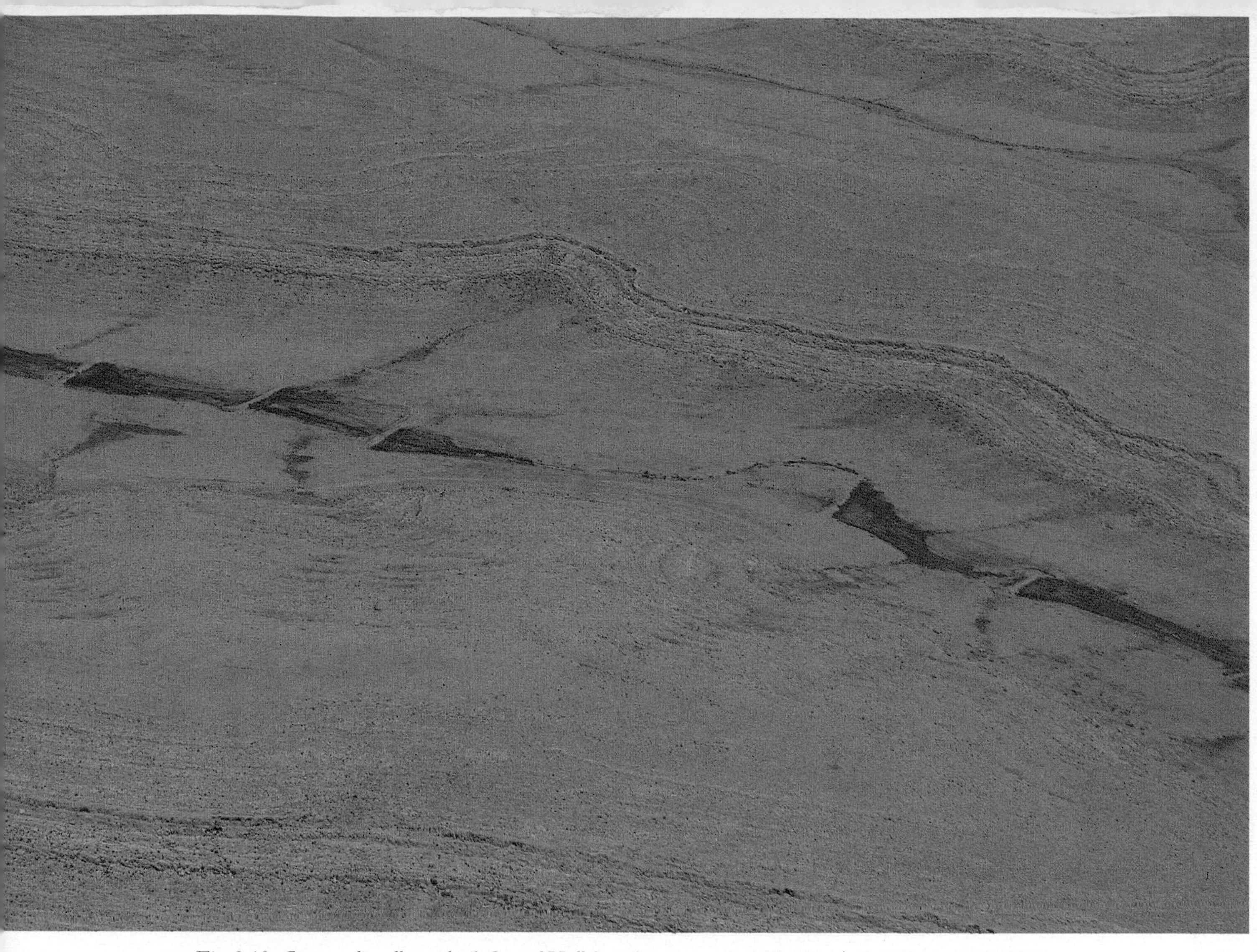

Fig. 2.12: Cross wadi walls north of Qasr el-Hallabat after winter rain (APA02.1/ SL7.29, 1 April 2002)

fewer people still. We may crudely estimate that Jarash at its peak in the Roman period had an urban population of *c.* 5,000–10,000. Most people however, even at the height of ancient urbanism, lived on the land, so that the territory of a place like Jarash may have had four times as many people as the city — ie 20,000 to 40,000. In medieval and early modern times, populations shrank as urban centres collapsed or declined to mere villages and nomadism, with its much lower population possibilities, dominated lands where once farmers supported much larger numbers. That all changed dramatically in the 20th century with a steady and now a steep increase in numbers through both immigration and a high birth rate.

Fig. 2.11: A dry wadi in the Hisma Desert south of Quweira (APA98/ SL41.11, 20 May 1998)

3. HISTORY

In the beginning ...

The earliest traces of humankind are to be found in Africa and much later in the Middle East. Jordan is relatively slow to produce evidence of our species — a mere 450,000 years ago! Subsequent development was painfully slow for hundreds of millennia and sites of this period have left few traces, even after excavation. Sites from more recent periods are better preserved. The human occupation of the region was not a linear progression, but marked by peaks and declines. There is good evidence of early nomadic intensive use, especially in the eastern desert, where migrating gazelle were followed, trapped and hunted on a very large scale (see Ch. 5). In the Early Bronze Age there was a peak in population and settlement, which left behind numerous substantial sites. More impressive still, was the increase in population in the Roman and early Umayyad periods, for which there are more sites than any other. A decline in population set in thereafter and, despite phases of great activity and recovery, the region became remote and remained undeveloped until the late 19th century. It would have been emptier still, but for the attractions of the arable lands of the northwest and the presence of the Pilgrim Road running the length of the country. Changes set in with the reforms of the later Ottoman Empire, the Turkish Republic and the construction of the Hejaz Railway. But it was only after 1919 that the country began to see population levels and a spread of settlement that was comparable to the high tide mark of the Roman period.

How do we know what happened in Jordan in the past? For more recent periods and for the early civilizations in the region we have written evidence — literature, archival documents on clay tablets or papyri, inscriptions, coin legends and seals are all available in varying quantities. But overwhelmingly the evidence available today is archaeological; indeed, for the earliest prehistoric periods it is all we have and even for much of history there is little written information. Archaeological evidence in Jordan, as elsewhere, is the outcome of three processes. First, excavation, traditionally regarded as the hallmark of archaeology. The better excavations provide detailed evidence of places, structures, everyday life, external contacts, technology, climate and most importantly, a chronology. Excavations produce huge quantities of evidence which takes years to analyse and synthesize. Second and more recently the technique of ground survey has been developed. At its simplest it consists of exploring extensive areas of land on foot, to record sites of every period, to define their size and character and, from surface artefacts collected, to provide some dating evidence. The technique has become immensely successful, popular and important; Jordan has been subject to more high quality archaeological surveys than any country in the entire eastern Mediterranean. Its contribution has been to show how intensively the landscape was used in the past, to emphasize just how numerous sites of every period are and to allow scholars to create maps showing the numbers and distribution of sites of each major period. Finally, as this book attests, there is aerial reconnaissance and photography. It too, allows us to populate the landscape. It can do this very effectively and over huge areas, but it needs ground work to confirm and date the sites found. Nevertheless, as described in Chapter 4, the 'productivity' of the technique can be quite overwhelming — *c.* 25,000 sites identified on air photographs of western Jordan alone.

The Palaeolithic (before 450,000–10,300 bp)

The entire duration of human history in Jordan occupies an immensely long period of several hundred thousand years but, as elsewhere, the great majority of this belongs to prehistory. Indeed it belongs to what used to be called the Old Stone Age which only ended about 12,000 years ago.

There are few explored sites of the Lower Palaeolithic and most of those are in the Azraq Basin where conditions were far wetter in the distant past. Although the population consisted mainly of small roving bands of 10–15 people, hunting and gathering, there is some evidence from southern Jordan that populations could combine on occasion to prey on migrating animals.

Middle Palaeolithic sites are far more numerous but there is a decline again in the Upper Palaeolithic. Site types are often no more than temporary camps, there are however a few with evidence of long occupation; one even has successive floors within a structure, while some sites in the Azraq Basin have material extending over 2 ha/ 5 acres.

The Neolithic and Chalcolithic (10,300 bp –3600 BC)

The Neolithic (or New Stone Age), characterized by the introduction of agriculture and a more settled sedentary way of life, usually sees the beginning of

Fig. 2.13: The Wadi Mushash after the winter rains (APA02.1/ SL2.3, 1 April 2002)

pottery manufacture, but in this region there is a 'Pre-Pottery Neolithic' period which saw dramatic transformations. The beginnings of agriculture and the domestication of animals went hand in hand with rising populations, different (rectangular) shapes in buildings, and striking ritual practices. In particular, a number of farming villages appeared. Some have been excavated and become household names amongst prehistorians. Ain Ghazal is the best known, but there are others in Jordan at Wadi Shu'eib, Beidha (Fig. 5.1) and Basta (Fig. 5.2), all of which stand out as being so much larger than anything seen before — *c.* 12 ha/ 30 acres. At Ain Ghazal early evidence for Neolithic religion and cult practices is suggested, not only in the way in which the dead were disposed of, but more remarkably still, in the clay figurines excavated.

Even with relatively small populations there is evidence for the removal of tree cover and the alteration of habitats that followed. It is now too, that humankind began to alter the landscape in a still more dramatic fashion with the construction of 'kites' used for trapping animals in the Basalt Desert (Fig. 5.4).

As the name implies, the Pottery Neolithic saw the first appearance of pottery on sites. At the same time, the number of sites increases, with many of these being perhaps the first villages.

There was a further surge in the number and scale of sites in the Chalcolithic (or Copper Age, a transitional period between the Neolithic and Bronze Age): a few have been excavated extensively in Jordan. The most famous is Teleilat el-Ghassul (Fig. 5.3) in the Jordan Valley just north of the Dead Sea, with another at Abu Hamid in the northern Jordan Valley.

The Bronze Age (3600–1200 BC)

The hallmark of the Bronze Age everywhere in the Near East is the appearance for the first time of towns. In contrast to the large villages of earlier periods we can now define urban centres, often marked very graphically on the modern landscape by the great artificial mounds formed from the accumulation of settlement over many generations (Figs 6.5, 6.6, 6.8; cf. 7.1). Jordan can boast numerous examples — most are in the Jordan Valley and the northwest; there are few in the south.

The pattern also varies through time. As the Chronological Table shows (above), the period is subdivided and subdivided again. The peak of urbanization is in what is called Early Bronze II and III. But it was not just the urban centres; most of the bigger settlements are small towns or big villages. Ground survey has revealed hundreds of even smaller sites. The distribution pattern does not include the far south, where there are few sites south of the Wadi el-Hasa, but it does include the seemingly inhospitable Basalt Desert of the northeast (Fig. 6.1). In fact, pollen analysis has indicated wetter conditions in this period and that may have provided an early stimulus to exploiting seemingly unattractive areas.

For the first time there are monumental buildings, some that can be called temples and 'palaces', and there are great defensive walls. Houses are usually of a courtyard type. Beyond the urban centres are some strikingly large cemeteries, but the period is most graphically illustrated in the wider landscape by the great 'fields' of dolmens, megalithic tombs, which strew the hillsides of northwestern and west central Jordan in particular.

The basis of the economy is still agriculture, of course, and the urban centres are situated close to the better soils and water resources of the Jordan Valley and northwestern highlands. The types of house favoured reflect this centralization as farmers concentrated their homes in towns rather than living in dispersed farms. There is one dramatic exception — the remarkable Bronze Age town of Jawa in the Basalt Desert (Fig. 6.1). The town overlooks a medium-sized wadi whose water was systematically 'harvested', but its isolation and uniqueness suggests it had a singular purpose, which has yet to be determined.

The Iron Age (1200–300 BC)

The Late Bronze Age saw first a break in settlement, then some urban sites re-occupied, and finally a spate of new sites appeared. Most of these continued into the Iron Age. It was in the Iron Age, for the first time, that we can start to assign names to groups of what appear to be nomadic tribes becoming sedentary and being identified in the ancient written sources (especially the Old Testament).

The outcome of progressive sedentarization throughout Jordan was the creation of definable states. Not centralized states as was once thought but looser arrangements for what are now described as 'tribal kingdoms'. Ammon, Moab and Edom dominate much of Jordan; rulers are named and interstate relations are described. Wars with the Israelites are recorded as the latter expanded east of the Jordan.

The states enjoyed a period of prosperity which reached a peak in what archaeologists define as Iron Age II. Some evidence comes from written sources and archaeological surveys have recorded hundreds of sites of this period. In the kingdom of Ammon, numerous towers and tombs in the Amman area have been recorded which date to this period. Moab in particular prospered and developed. The Mesha Inscription is a basalt stele recording the achievements of the 9th

century BC ruler of a kingdom centred on Dibon (Fig. 7.2). Archaeologically striking are the Moabite border fortresses which seem to have been created to define and protect the boundaries of the emergent state. Several have been excavated (Figs 7.7, 7.8) as has Dibon itself. But there are also hundreds of other sites of Iron II in this region. In the south, the character of Edomite settlement has been revealed by excavation at such urban sites as Buseirah, Tawilan and Umm el-Biyara. Many associated smaller farming settlements have also been discovered. Once again, however, this most southerly part of Jordan seems the most thinly settled.

In the 8th century BC the region largely fell under the control of distant overlords: first the Assyrians, then the Babylonians and finally the Persians, all of them empires centred in what is now Iraq and Iran. The Iron Age II vassal kingdoms of Jordan seem to have collapsed in the 6th century BC as Persian rule replaced Babylonian. The numbers of Persian period sites is very small and artefacts of the period are very scarce. The impression is of a widespread reversion to nomadism, a shrinkage of settlement and loss of effective imperial control over all but the most fertile parts of northwest Jordan. It may have been towards the end of this period, that the Persian satrap of this large province of Syria, installed the Jewish Tobiad family in the western part of Ammon to rule it on his behalf (Fig. 9.1).

The Hellenistic, Hasmonaean and Herodian period (332 BC–1st century AD)

Persian rule of Jordan ended in 332 BC with the arrival of Alexander the Great and his annexation of all of the Persian satrapies in the Near East. The wars that followed his death in 323, led to the creation of two Hellenistic Greek kingdoms in the region, which warred over control of Jordan. The Ptolemaic kings of Egypt ruled over the northern part of Jordan and Palestine for a century. Then it passed to the Seleucid kings of Syria, whose rule lasted a further century before it too, began to disintegrate. First the Seleucids lost Palestine to the Hasmonaeans in the 2nd century and progressively the latter extended their rule beyond the Jordan as well. The same period saw the revival of a sedentarized state in the south, the Nabataeans, who expanded their rule northwards and who were credited with control of even Damascus. Then Tigranes the Great of Armenia overran the remnants of the entire Seleucid kingdom. When the armies of the Roman general Pompey the Great, arrived in the Near East in the mid-60s BC, they drove out Armenians and others, but did not restore the Seleucid kingdom. Instead, a Roman province of Syria was created and adjacent territories were placed in the hands of allied rulers. The most notable of these were the successive Jewish rulers in the southwest. First the Hasmonaeans were confirmed by Rome, then in the 30s and 20s BC, Herod the Great was installed as king, first by Mark Antony and then by the Emperor Augustus, who gave him extensive territories east of the Jordan and Lake Tiberias.

The territories in question had become partly Hellenized during this period, starting in the later 3rd century. In the northwest of Jordan, southern Syria and just west of the River Jordan, a number of cities appeared, known collectively as the Decapolis (although, confusingly, the full list of names is greater than ten). Most were at places which had been urban in the Bronze Age and Iron II periods. Now however, they have 'Greek' names and an emerging Hellenistic culture. In Jordan the key places are Abila, Gadara, Pella, Gerasa and Philadelphia; at all of which there has been extensive excavation (Figs 9.3–9.6, 11.2).

The Nabataeans (300 BC–AD 106)

The earliest references to the Nabataeans show them settled in southern Jordan, southeast of the Dead Sea, in the 4th century BC. They were already attracting predatory attention. One of Alexander's generals made a raid in 312 BC to try and seize their fabled wealth, but it ended badly as his forces encountered the harsh conditions and difficult terrain of the mountainous lands around Petra. Their subsequent early history is problematic, but they were evidently developing in three ways: first, becoming increasingly settled as part of the population shifted away from nomadism; second, becoming prosperous on the caravan trade through their region; and third expanding their sphere of influence and control. Already we hear of kings in the 2nd century BC and by the 1st century we can confidently assign names and dates to these rulers.

The Nabataeans emerge as a significant regional power in the 1st century BC. Their capital of Petra became an architectural wonder and many of the best-known monuments and buildings there are now known to belong to this prosperous period before the Roman annexation. They appear in more distant parts of the region with inscriptions in their own language, while their distinctive pottery and monuments are found widely: to the south in the Hejaz Province of northwest Saudi Arabia, far to the east in the Wadi Sirhan and at the great oasis of Jauf in the Northern Province of Saudi Arabia, west across the Negev Desert and in the north where they developed the steppe lands of the Hauran and created a new northern capital at Bostra, thus creating a kingdom extending from the Hauran to the Red Sea, the Mediterranean to the Arabian Desert.

Nomadism remained a strong feature of Nabataean society, but their kingdom was one of cities, small towns, hundreds of agricultural villages and still more numerous farms. Although it was heavily influenced by the Hellenistic-Roman world all around, it retained an impressive, attractive and above all distinctive culture. Petra is the obvious example (Figs 8.1A–C) but there are also important religious sites (Figs 8.2–8.4) and its art and artefacts are rightly renowned.

There were wars between Nabataeans and Herodians, and Roman armies were launched on punitive expeditions to bring this remote 'ally' to heel. Finally, in AD 106, Roman forces annexed the Nabataean kingdom. Three of the Decapolis cities of southern Syria — Adraha, Gerasa and Philadelphia — were detached and added to the former kingdom, to form a new province with the resonant name of Arabia.

Early Rome (64 BC–AD 324)

Roman involvement in Jordan began with Pompey the Great in the 60s BC when his forces operated east of the Jordan and in southern Syria. The 'Greek' cities of the Decapolis were treated in different ways — some were given to Herod and his successors; others were placed under direct Roman administration as part of the province of Syria. In the case of those in northern Jordan, Gerasa and Philadelphia were certainly part of Roman Syria, while Gadara and Pella were not. It was only after the creation of Provincia Arabia in AD 106 that the position was formalized: Gadara and Pella belonged to the province of Judaea (soon renamed Syria Palaestina) and Gerasa and Philadelphia to Arabia. Both Judaea and Arabia were middle-rank military provinces with legions in garrison, though none of these were headquartered in Jordan itself, but at Caparcotna and Jerusalem, and Bostra respectively. However, there were citizen legionaries and provincial auxiliaries in what is now Jordan; we have references to them in some of the Decapolis cities and in detachments elsewhere in Jordan. Arabia as a whole had a garrison of about 10,000 soldiers and perhaps half of those would have been based in Jordan. Forts are still quite rare in this period because most troops were probably billeted in the cities; but there are a few examples (Fig. 10.3).

After the annexation of Nabataea in AD 106, Bostra was made the capital of the province of Arabia and became a legionary base. But Petra continued to prosper, as did towns and villages in that area. In the northwest, the Decapolis cities underwent a long period of development extending over the 1st and 2nd centuries AD. The result was dramatic: the small Hellenistic cities grew, streets were laid out, monumental buildings appeared — temples, theatres, circuses, bath buildings etc. In fact the Decapolis cities are famous for the size and number of these public buildings (Figs 9.3–9.6). Populations included people with Greek ancestors and there are examples of retired Roman soldiers; most, however, were simply the native population adopting Graeco-Roman names and culture, modified to suit their own tastes and needs. This was even more true of the smaller, less 'Greek' cities of the region — Madaba (Fig. 11.1B), Hesban, Er-Rabbah (Fig. 9.8), Characmoab (cf. Fig. 13.1) — and still more so with the towns.

Outside the towns large cemeteries grew up and many include impressive monumental tombs (Figs 9.9A–B), some of these still preserving elaborate wall paintings underground.

Beyond the cities, the Roman authorities built roads and bridges (Fig. 9.10B). Most famous was the great highway of the Emperor Trajan (AD 98–117) stretching from Syria to Aqaba on the Red Sea, the *Via Nova Traiana* (Fig. 9.10A). Numerous others, marked by tall milestones, created a network throughout the province. The countryside developed too, and the number of sites recorded in ground surveys for this period rises significantly.

Late Rome (AD 324–640)

The later 3rd and 4th centuries AD saw changes taking place. In chronological order these are: the building of military structures, a growth in the number and spread of settlements of all kinds, and the proliferation of a new religious structure. In administration, the province of Arabia had its boundaries adjusted on a number of occasions. Then, in the later 3rd century, as smaller provinces became the norm across the entire empire, it was split in half: the north remained Arabia and the south became Palaestina Tertia.

Jordan can boast some of the best-preserved forts anywhere in the entire Roman Empire. Rectangular or square, stone-built and sturdy, with tall walls and projecting towers, they became a distinctive feature of the eastern part of the province where settled farmer met nomad (Ch. 10 and Figs 11.3 and 11.6). It is, as yet, difficult to disentangle the sequence of events. What we can say is that new forts appear in the 3rd century AD, there is a spate of additional building around AD 300 and more again in the 4th century. Many of the forts are in the steppe lands of the northeast, or along the fringes of the desert. In this same period the steppe lands sprout numerous new settlements and existing villages develop into small towns (Fig. 11.3). The Basalt Desert of the northeast also saw an increase in human settlement.

One of the problems yet to be resolved, is whether the forts permitted and stimulated settlement, or if the growing settlements drew in the army to police and protect. There is certainly abundant evidence for new settlements in large numbers throughout the province (Figs 11.3, 11.4, 11.5, 11.6 and 11.8).

The cities had acquired most of the great public buildings that characterize them, but the beginnings of Christianity as a force stimulated new building types in the landscape. Churches appear in cities, towns and villages: large numbers of them — 15 in Gerasa alone, with equal numbers even in some of the smaller towns (Figs 11.1–11.6). Hundreds are known in Jordan. Some were built in and over old temples (Fig. 8.2) but most are new buildings and architecturally different from what went before. They often include lavish mosaic floors, some with inscriptions naming a bishop and the date of construction. The best examples belong to the 6th and 7th centuries (continuing after the Islamic conquest) when church building and mosaics are most numerous (Fig. 11.6).

This Late Roman period saw more settlement and more of almost everything, than at any period since the Bronze Age and — very remarkably — more than we find ever again in Jordan until the 20th century. Artefacts are striking by their number, range, quality and often distant origins — everything survives in larger numbers than at any other pre-modern period: settlements, coins, pottery, lamps, glass, metalwork, inscriptions, bones, ... It is a remarkable testimony to the 'modernity' of the Roman world, a forerunner of the great consumer and polluter states of the present.

The Umayyad period (AD 640–750)

The Islamic armies' invasion of Jordan encountered a 'Roman' population. By the 6th century people there were overwhelmingly Christian. They had all long been granted Roman citizenship and had been part of the Roman Mediterranean world for several hundred years. They could look back on generations of continuity and development, and of being a component of a seemingly invulnerable universal state.

But the Roman Empire proved vulnerable in the early 7th century. Key battles were fought in Jordan — at Mutah south of Kerak and Fihl (Pella) (Fig. 9.5), while the decisive Battle of the Yarmuk (AD 636) was just beyond that river in southwestern Syria. At the latter, the forces of Islam crushed the Roman army and went on to annexe all of the eastern Roman provinces as far as the north of Syria, before overthrowing the entire Sassanian Empire to its east. A new Islamic Empire was established under the Umayyad dynasty, with its first caliph in 661. Ultimately the Umayyads created an empire stretching from Spain to Central Asia. Most importantly for Jordan, it was centred at Damascus, just a short distance north, a dramatic change after centuries of distant capitals. Jordan, from Jarash northwards, formed much of the new military district called Al-Urdunn, while the remainder, stretching in an arc around the east of the highlands, through Amman and south to, but not including Aqaba — which belonged to Egypt — was the province of Damascus.

The centrality of northern Jordan to the new empire, probably explains the string of at least 10 rich residences the Umayyads and their vassals built in the steppe and desert areas. Rural retreats with mosques, baths and carefully managed 'gardens' (Figs 4.11, 10.4, 12.2, 12.4–12.7). At one time it was thought that Islamic rule had brought a rapid decline and the ultimate collapse of the urban life, population and prosperity of the Roman period. We now know there was widespread continuity everywhere, even, for many years, in the pottery types of the Late Roman period. In Amman, the local Muslim governor constructed his residence on the Graeco-Roman citadel and the ancient placename Rabbath-Ammon reappears; perhaps the name had never been entirely lost amongst the native and rural population of what had been Philadelphia — the thousand years of its Classical history a mere episode in a far older culture. In a few places new mosques were built and some churches were converted to mosques, but many churches contain mosaics with dates of the early Islamic period and general construction continued in towns. Ground surveys show numerous rural sites still occupied in this period. One notable change is that while grape cultivation continued, wine production facilities became less common on many rural farms.

The new dynasty was eclectic. It made use of much of what it found, as well as borrowing architecturally from both Sassanian Persia (Fig. 12.1) and Rome (Fig. 12.8). Early art included the human form, as in the marvellous wall paintings at Qusayr Amra (Fig. 12.4). Later however, such paintings disappear. This was part of an iconoclasm that affected Christians too: we find even existing mosaics still on display, having human forms removed and replaced, as a prohibition on the human form became the norm in both Islam and Christianity.

Jordan had long lain on a network of trade routes, and these continued and flourished in an empire that spanned much more of their length. Now however, traffic also moved in the other direction too, as many pilgrims passed through on their way to Mecca.

The Abbasid and Fatimid periods (AD 750–1071)

Although the Umayyad dynasty survived and flourished in Spain for some centuries longer, it lost its empire in North Africa and the Middle East to a new dynasty in the mid-8th century. The Abbasid family owned an estate at Humayma in southern Jordan (Fig. 10.3) and plotted its revolt there but, after seizing power, it shifted the seat of government eastwards from Damascus to a new capital at Baghdad. The impact in Jordan is visible in the decline of the rural retreats and the general contraction in the extent of settlement. The towns continued but in more limited form and the numbers of sites of the period in the wider landscape is far fewer.

The shift of the political centre of gravity was one explanation; another was the effect in the 9th century of raids by a new tribal group, the Tayy', which disrupted settlement. At the same time, local political forces achieved a measure of autonomy and eventually in 969, a new rival Fatimid caliphate established itself in Egypt and took control of the western part of the Abbasid Empire. Henceforth, a combination of weaker political control and nomadic raids brought a decline in settlement size, number and extent. Documentary sources record disruption of the pilgrimage in Jordan and we may suppose that trade was affected too.

This was a world of rapid change. Further north, the Byzantine Empire almost collapsed in the face of advances into Asia Minor by powerful Turkic groups and the shrinking world of Christendom was removed still further from Jordan. The instability in Syria and Jordan, and weakness of political control, were to add to the factors which lay behind the next major phase.

But we should not exaggerate the supposed decline. Writing about AD 985, the Arab geographer al-Muqaddasi, described Jordan in terms that implies a prosperity and vigour at odds with the traditional image of decline and the thin evidence recorded by archaeologists. But the latter is largely because few archaeologists were, until recently, interested: Al-Muqaddasi in contrast, enumerates at least 8 significant centres, numerous villages, widespread cultivation of olives, grapes, grain and the rearing of flocks, as well as important trade in the south at Wayla (Aqaba) and the regional capital of Sughar (Zoar) at the head of the Wadi Araba. This was the world into which western armies now intruded so violently.

The Crusader (AD 1099–1291); **the Ayyubid and Mamluk periods** (1174–1516)

Despite recent upheavals in the region, the appearance of the first armies of westerners in 1099 was a great shock to the peoples of the Near East. The frightful savagery and massacres allowed the establishment of Frankish principalities in an arc from north-western Mesopotamia down the coast of the Levant to the Red Sea, including a slice of western Jordan. They were not to endure, despite brief episodes of reinforcement and recovery. The Muslim reaction and reconquest, and the subsequent Mongol invasions drove the region into further decline.

Two dramatic effects on the archaeological record are evident. First is the sharp decline in the number of sites occupied in Jordan and the small size of those that remained. Dating is a problem however: there are signs that some decline pre-dated the Crusades, and that in places the latter may have arrested the process. Second is the appearance of a new military architecture. The Crusader Kingdom of Jerusalem established massive castles throughout the kingdom and in time these spread into Jordan, as the king seized control of the western strip of the country from the Dead Sea to the Gulf of Aqaba (Figs 13.1–13.3).

When control began to be re-established by the Muslims, first under the vigorous Zangid family and then the Ayyubid dynasty of the famous Saladin (Salah ad-Din al-Ayyubi), Islamic castles were founded in turn (Fig. 13.4). But the wars had further disrupted trade and the pilgrimage to Mecca and Medina and had driven routes further east. There, another work of fortification was established to control the desert route through the Wadi Sirhan to Arabia (Fig. 13.5).

In 1260 a Mongol army was defeated and turned back at the decisive battle of 'Ain Jalut, south of Nazareth; in 1291 the last part of the Kingdom of Jerusalem was eliminated and the Frankish incursion was over. The credit for these successes was due to the soldier slaves, who came to power as the new Mamluk dynasty based on Egypt. Archaeology has revealed traces of revival in this period — settlement in the Jordan Valley and central and northern Jordan, and renewed mining in the Wadi Araba (Fig. 11.10). Literary sources show flourishing communities at specific places — Ajlun, Hesban, Kerak, Shaubak — and the main Pilgrim Road could shift westwards again, to a line along the King's Highway (cf. Figs 13.7 and 14.1). But this was a limited prosperity compared with the past — Amman, for example, was avoided by pilgrims and said to be in ruins.

The Ottoman Empire

The Crusades were meant to recover the Christian holy places in the Near East, but led instead to the complete loss of all Christian control there and the collapse of the remaining Christian powers in Western Asia. After the losses in the Levant itself, the Kingdom of Armenia and its Frankish dynasty was overthrown in 1375; in 1426 the Mamluks devastated the Crusader Kingdom of Cyprus; in 1453 the Ottoman Turks captured Constantinople and soon eliminated the remnants of the Byzantine Empire; in 1517 Egypt fell to the Ottomans; and in 1523 it was the turn of the Hospitaller island fortress of Rhodes.

Christian communities survived in the Near East, including Jordan (especially at Madaba and Kerak) but the long episode of the Crusades altered the religious map of the entire eastern Mediterranean and left the great urban centres — including Jerusalem — mere shadows of their former importance. The Ottomans were not the cause of the ruin of the Near East, but they did little to revive it.

Jordan remained a crucial area on the pilgrim route. The earlier efforts of the Mamluks were revived and developed by the Ottoman sultans, sometimes reconstructing existing places but also some new sites. Outstanding was the work of Suleiman the Magnificent (AD 1520–1566) who shifted the route eastwards to the edge of the desert. The old King's Highway continued to be used, but now forts and protected reservoirs marked the line of the modern Desert Highway (Figs 14.2–14.3). There were Ottoman forts elsewhere, too — not just the great castles of the preceding period, but new posts at Udruh and perhaps Khirbat edh-Dusaq east of Shaubak. In the northwest and along the edge of the scarp, above the Jordan and Dead Sea, settlements survived alongside springs and streams, while the ruined watermills of this Ottoman period are a feature still, of the modern landscape (Fig. 14.5B). In the early 20th century the Hejaz Railway was constructed to carry pilgrims along the desert's edge. The line is still there and some of it still in use. The railway stations survive much as they were built (Fig. 14.6).

Ottoman documents have been exploited in recent years, to show the extent to which the land of Jordan was being used for farming in the later 19th century, as security was restored then extended, with Circassian communities settled in such places as Salt (Fig. 14.5B), Jarash and Amman. New villages appeared and a few have been preserved as mementoes of a period, now being overgrown by rapid modern development (Figs 14.5A and 14.9B). Traveller's reports of the 19th century leave little doubt, however, that the Ottoman writ was effective only in their major administrative centres — Salt, Kerak, Ma'an, Aqaba — and stopped on the edge of a narrow settled area. Beduin controlled the thinly populated land beyond and left their mark in seasonal camps at water holes and along transhumance routes. They also routinely penetrated deep into the settled areas and even beyong the River Jordan.

During the First World War Transjordan was freed from Turkish control by what is known as the Arab Revolt, made famous in books — especially T.E. Lawrence's *Seven Pillars of Wisdom* — and the cinema. The Arab forces were working in tandem with British imperial forces, both in Palestine and in Transjordan. The traces of battles are still to be seen in places in Jordan, not least in the Turkish trenches, still visible over 80 years later, at strong points they chose to defend (Fig. 14.7A). The final attack in 1918 began with the concentration of the Arab Army at the Azraq Oasis (Fig. 13.5).

The British Mandate

The San Remo Conference (1920) divided the Turkish provinces of the Near East between Britain and France as 'mandates', territories which they were deputed to develop and bring to independence under their tutelage. The British share was divided into Iraq, Palestine and Transjordan. In an odd quirk of post-war politics, in Transjordan and Iraq (but not Palestine) a case was made, and accepted, for creating military commands which were presided over by officers of the newly formed Royal Air Force. The rationale being that relatively unpopulated and undeveloped lands, or broken terrain, could be policed effectively — and cheaply — by a few aircraft able to roam everywhere (and use bombing as a deterrent against revolt) and backed up by detachments of RAF armoured cars and native auxiliary forces. Transjordan became an Air Force Command, with aircraft established at some of the bases from which German pilots had been operating only a few months before — and from which they photographed numerous archaeological sites (Ch. 4). One of those bases was just northeast of Amman, on the plateau just above the Hejaz Railway station of Marka; it later became Jordan's first international airport and Marka is still today a civil and military airfield (Fig. 14.8A). Another airfield was developed near the Roman reservoir, Ottoman hajj fort and Hejaz railway station at Jiza; it became a staging point on the Cairo to the Persian Gulf route, blazed by the RAF in 1926 (Fig. 14.1B). It is now lost beneath the Queen Alia International Airport, but the other stopping points and the measures taken to guide pilots across the desert to Iraq, are still often visible (Fig. 14.8B).

Alongside the RAF were formed the Transjordan Frontier Force and the Arab Legion, to police the country in general and the desert areas in particular. Forts for them were built throughout the country, many of which survive intact (Fig. 14.7B).

The Hashemite Kingdom

In 1921 the British created a state for the Amir (later King) Abdullah, whose brother Feisal had led the Arab Revolt. Transjordan was to be self-governing under the supervision of a High Commissioner, assisted by British officers in the military units. In 1928 the Organic Law took the process further and in 1939 control was effectively passed to the Amir (King Abdullah I) with Britain retaining military bases. It is thanks to the support of King Abdullah's grandson (Prince el-Hassan) and great-grandson (Prince Feisal) that this book was made possible.

Salt (Fig. 14.5B) had been the seat of government in Ottoman times, but under British control that soon shifted to Amman. The latter has been transformed in the last century, from a small town of 2–3,000 people living around the ruins of imperial Rome and the Umayyad palace on the citadel, into the immense city of today with major public buildings (Fig. 9.3) and a population of (2002) *c.* 1.9 million people. Jordan too, has developed swiftly with new roads, towns, settlements of all kinds and a rapidly growing threat to the archaeological heritage. Places that had been remote and impressive ruins in 1900 were confronted with new agriculture and rising populations with urgent demands. At its best, archaeology and present needs combine harmoniously (Fig. 14.5B); but archaeology can also be at the mercy of development (Fig. 9.4). The role of aerial archaeology is important here and is discussed in the next chapter.

4. SEEING FROM THE AIR

The Aerial View

Origins

The principle of aerial survey is simple: from a high vantage point you can get a more comprehensive and intelligible view of the landscapes below. Armies knew this long ago and when hot air balloons were developed in the 19th century, it was not long before generals were sending their scouts aloft to spy on enemy positions. The invention of the camera allowed flying to be combined with photography, to produce permanent records of what the aerial observer was seeing. Despite early proposals for applying both to archaeology, the first major (but unrealized) project was that of the British Army's Balloon Unit in 1891, to use a balloon and camera to photograph and then map the 50 ha of the deserted Moghul city of Fatehpur Sikri in India. In 1906 Stonehenge became the first archaeological site in Britain to be photographed from the air. Soon after, World War I gave an enormous impetus to aerial observation and photography, as all the protagonists took to the air and carried out extensive reconnaissance in all the major theatres of operation.

Some of the men involved in wartime turned their knowledge to peacetime uses. Foremost was O.G.S. Crawford, the acknowledged 'father' of aerial archaeology and founder of the archaeological periodical *Antiquity*. Crawford's contribution was to systematize the lessons of aerial reconnaissance and establish the technique of aerial archaeology.

The Technique

An aerial view can contribute to archaeological inquiry in various ways. First, is simply to get a novel view of the well known. It has become common for publications to include aerial views of archaeological sites, simply because they are so effective at showing graphically what a place or structure looks like in a single image. The 'bird's-eye view' provides an unique and invaluable insight, not just in the detail of the site, but in its landscape context. From above we can see, not just the site, but where it is in a landscape and perhaps infer why it is there: the military structure on the top of the tallest hill, the town at the junction of rivers or routes, the village on the edge of rich soils.

But aerial archaeology soon went beyond looking at the known and broadly intelligible sites. Archaeologists discovered that from above, the jumble of collapsed walls or unintelligible earthworks could emerge as a pattern — the walls of buildings could be seen, the streets of settlements, the outline of collapsed fortifications.

Sometimes such revelations were simply a matter of getting above the site to see clearly. Increasingly, however, archaeologists discovered that sites showed better at certain times: low slanting sunlight in the early morning or later in the day cast shadows and made the outlines of structures sharper and clear. They had discovered 'shadow sites'.

The next step was the discovery of sites that had *no* remains on the surface. We are now very familiar with the startling contrast between the photograph of a field, which appears flat and entirely featureless at ground level and the revelation in an aerial view of the traces that survive beneath the surface. Once again it is timing that is the key. Each year as farmers plough their fields, they may be cutting into the tops of buried archaeological features. The dark soil of a long filled-in ditch, or rubble from a wall foundation, will be brought to the surface. For a short time, these 'soilmarks' will be visible from the air and can show the shape and form of what lies beneath the surface. The third type of revelation is the one most people are familiar with. In spring and summer, crops will often have their growth pattern affected by what lies beneath the surface. The richer soils and moisture of a filled-in ditch accelerate growth and ripening, and produce 'cropmarks'; the obstacle of buried walls and lack of moisture around them have the opposite effect. Cropmarks have revealed in great detail, many thousands of archaeological features, structures and the plans of entire settlements.

Types of Photograph

There are two main types of aerial photograph, which archaeologists use to make records of archaeological sites — verticals and obliques.

Vertical aerial photographs are taken by cameras which have been mounted inside aircraft so that large areas of land below can be photographed automatically. Vertical photographs are usually under-taken for non-archaeological purposes and are not usually for recording archaeological sites, but all the resulting photographs still have to be assessed for their archaeological potential. The current campaign of aerial reconnaissance in Jordan, using **oblique photography**, was begun as a direct result of the discoveries from vertical photographs taken in 1953.

Fig. 4.1: The fort at Khirbat Ain (APA99/ SL16.25, 15 June 1999)

Vertical photographs tend to cover large areas and are especially useful for mapping or planning. Many millions of these exist around the world. For example, the National Monuments Record in England holds about four million vertical and oblique photographs, and the collection of wartime photographs (taken by the RAF over Europe) at Keele University runs to about three million.

Oblique aerial photography requires an altogether different approach from passive vertical surveys. The archaeologist-photographer has a purpose and a set of research questions in mind, before embarking on a flight or survey. Hand-held cameras are used (usually from the open window of a single-engined, high-wing aircraft or helicopter) to obtain the optimum view. The quality of this view will depend on the **angle of the sun**, **time of day**, **season** and **ground conditions**.

Most images of archaeological sites are oblique angle and taken from a low height. In this case the photograph has usually been taken by an archaeologist, flying in what is believed to be optimal conditions, and positioning the aircraft to get the best results. Once again there are now many millions of such oblique aerial photographs of archaeological sites.

Types of aircraft

Archaeologists have experimented with balloons big enough to carry the photographer or sometimes just to hold the camera; they have also employed a variety of kites; and work is going on in Armenia using a paramotor (a powered para-glider). Overwhelmingly however, the preferred 'platforms' are a fixed-wing aircraft, or a helicopter. Amongst aircraft types, preference is for a two or four seat aircraft, with a high wing. These are cheap to operate, manoeuvrable and the large window can be opened to allow a wide view. Helicopters are far more expensive to operate, but they have an enviable manoeuvrability and the ability to hover in an optimum position, also the entire door can be opened, giving about 140° of lateral view.

Achievements and Limitations

After less than a century, the achievements of aerial archaeology are astonishing. Many tens of thousands of sites have been found from the air. Entire landscapes once thought to contain little or nothing have emerged — not just strewn with sites of all kinds and periods, but with networks of roads and fields surrounding them. It is no exaggeration to say that the map of the

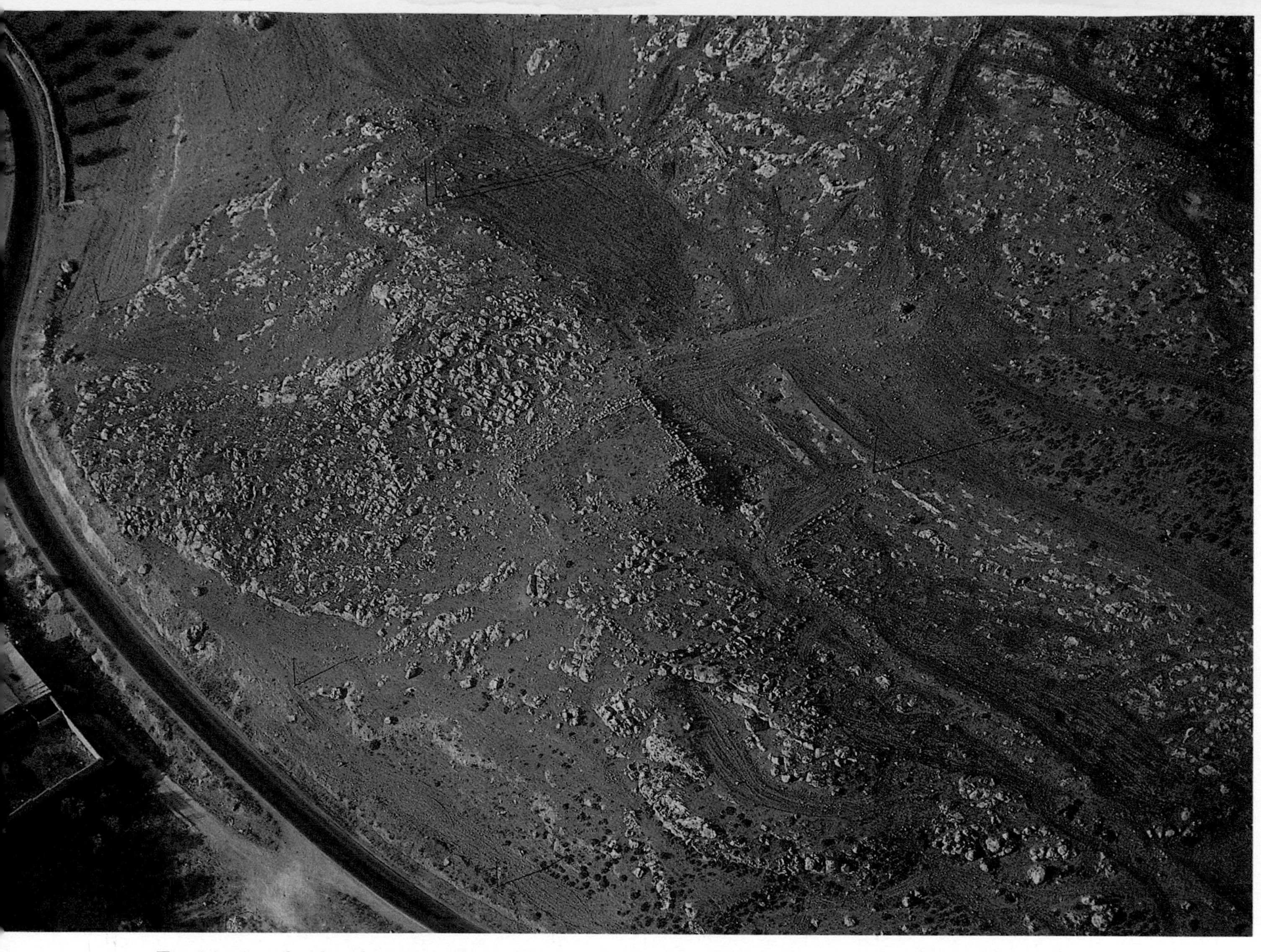

Fig. 4.2: A road and road-station at Khirbat Shereiyit 3 km southeast of Jarash (APA00/ SL3.10, 29 August 2000)

archaeology of much of western Europe in particular, has been transformed. In several European countries aerial archaeology has become a routine feature of the overall archaeological programme of research and it has spread swiftly into eastern Europe since the collapse of the Soviet empire.

The applications have become very diverse: illustrating our cultural heritage through evocative images; making permanent records of known sites; discovery of new sites and features; monitoring sensitive or vulnerable areas; and as a guide to ground work. In England and some other parts of Britain, aerial photographs are now the basis for ambitious projects to map and record all archaeological remains visible from the air. The resulting maps are used by archaeologists every day in helping them make decisions about which sites require further conservation or management.

There are of course limitations. Most existing photographs were taken for planning or mapping purposes rather than archaeology and the timing of the photography is not always suitable for archaeology. Conditions for discovery vary from year to year and the technique is not as predictable as one would like. Not every part of even the best-explored countries, such as Britain, is covered in equal detail by professionals and amateurs.

Above all however, after nearly a century, there are many countries which restrict access to existing air photograph collections and where it is illegal to fly, or photograph from the air, for archaeology at all. In short, one of the most productive and cost-effective techniques for prospection and interpretation, and a major weapon in the armoury of cultural resource management, is simply not available for many countries of the world. This is the case with most of the Middle East.

The Origins of Aerial Archaeology in Jordan

Pioneers

One of the revelations of recent years has been that aerial archaeology was underway in parts of the Middle East during World War I. Australian, British and French aviators took air photographs of archaeological sites there, but the major achievement was that of the Germans. They even had a Unit for the Protection of Monuments (Denkmalschutzkommando), under the archaeologist Theodor Wiegand, devoted to recording archaeological sites in the Negev desert. More than that,

Fig. 4.3: Ancient structures in the Basalt Desert south of Umm el-Jimal (APA98/ SL9.34, 12 May 1998)

however, amongst tens of hundreds of German air photographs surviving in official and private collections, are photographs of thousands of archaeological sites, in what was then Syria, Palestine and Transjordan, and landscapes now developed beyond recognition.

The Royal Air Force

After World War I, flying for archaeology was carried out more systematically in the region, in Syria in particular. There, the remarkable French Jesuit priest, Père Antoine Poidebard, was flown by the French Air Force to find and record ancient remains. The principal result was his profoundly evocative collection of images in a two-volume book — *La Trace de Rome* — published in 1934. Parallel efforts in the neighbouring British mandates were much more limited. First, came the work of individual pilots, confronted by the amazing tangle of sites they could see beneath them as they patrolled and flew the mail. Fl. Lt Maitland was encouraged to publish some of his findings in the very first issue of *Antiquity* in 1927 as "The Works of the Old Men' in Arabia'. Soon after, Group Captain Rees published further articles in *Antiquity* on other discoveries in Transjordan. Crawford himself, visited RAF bases in the region in 1928, with the intention of having the RAF routinely transfer him the redundant photographs they took each year. The key work here, however, was by the great orientalist and Central Asian explorer, Sir Aurel Stein. In 1938 and 1939 he flew with the RAF in Iraq and Transjordan to obtain the material for his *Limes Report* — his account of the Roman military installations in these two countries.

The Next Fifty Years

Despite these promising beginnings, progress largely ended after 1945. This was due partly to the emergence of newly independent countries and partly to the state of war in the region, which persists to this day. There were exceptions, not least in Jordan, where individuals were occasionally given flights to photograph archaeological sites. Jordan was always far more liberal than its neighbours — in the mid-1970s it was already possible to access the military archives for specific photographs and later, and very remarkably, they provided copy negatives of all 4,000 frames of a detailed vertical survey of western Jordan to one of the present authors (Kennedy). But, for active aerial archaeology — systematic and large scale flying and photography — our

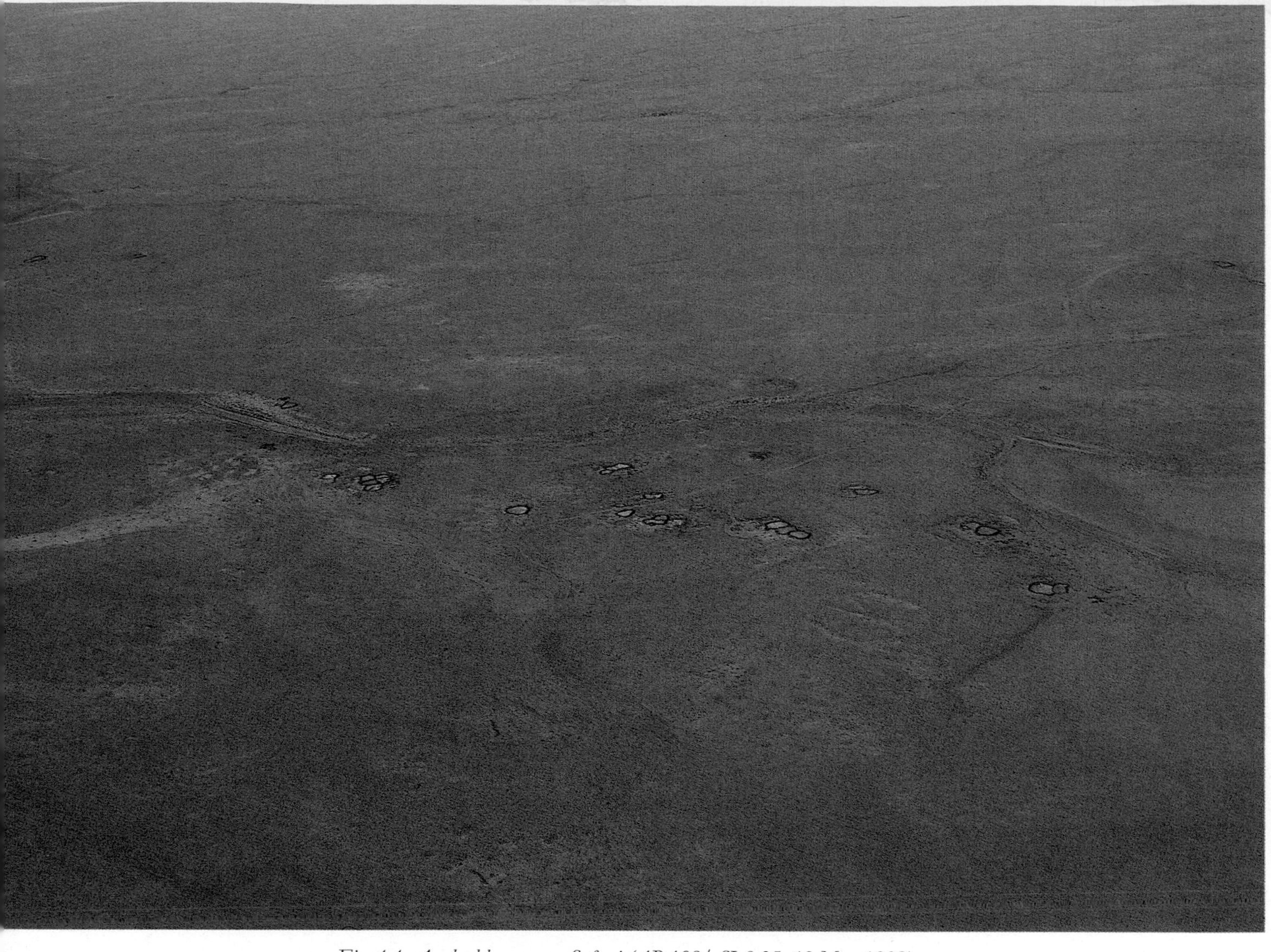

Fig. 4.4: A wheel house near Safawi (APA98/ SL8.25, 12 May 1998)

programme after 1997 was essentially picking up from where Sir Aurel Stein left off in 1939.

The Current Programme

The opportunity in the 1990s to carry out the detailed, systematic interpretation of some 4,000 vertical air photographs of western Jordan was of signal importance. The outcome was the identification of *c.* 25,000 'sites', three times the number recorded in the Jordanian Archaeological Database and Information System (JADIS). This exercise had been a major research project on air photographs and made Jordan virtually unique in the region.

There had been some flying to photograph archaeological sites in Israel over a long period and in 1990–1992, Derrick Riley, Ben Isaac and Mordechai Gichon carried out three brief seasons of systematic flying. That ended with Riley's death in 1995. Then, in 1997 the first of 8 seasons of intensive flying dedicated to archaeology was carried out in Jordan — the first of its kind in the Middle East for over half a century and a tribute to Jordan's openness.

The majority of photographs presented here were taken by the authors using hand held (usually Nikon) 35 mm cameras and a variety of film-types, either Fuji Reala (colour print film), Fuji Provia (transparency) and Ilford FP4. The normal aircraft employed was a Huey Helicopter (1997–1999; 2002–03), and on occasion an Aerospatial Super Puma (1998, 2003), a Britten-Norman Islander (2000) and a Cessna 152 (2001).

The Same But Different

The potential of aerial survey in Jordan is the same as elsewhere and it can be used for the same purposes. However, sites revealed by cropmarks and soilmarks are rare in Jordan. The vast majority of archaeological sites visible from the air are upstanding stoneworks or earthworks. Consequently, the major task of aerial survey for archaeology in Jordan is in locating such sites and making a good (and illustrative) record. The major requirement for making a good photographic record is the right lighting conditions in clear air. An immediate advantage is that such recording can be done all year round — weather conditions, rather than the stage in crop growth, being the crucial factor.

The present programme of aerial archaeology in Jordan was able to turn to three places for guidance. First, to the pioneering work of the 1920s and 30s, most

Fig. 4.5: A kite embedded in the modern landscape near Mukeifteh (APA98/ SL8.6, 12 May 1998)

particularly, the detailed discussion by Poidebard of the techniques and methods he developed in Syria. Second, the lessons learnt by Riley, Isaac and Gichon in Israel in the early 90s. Finally, the 80 years of development and increasing sophistication of the technique in Britain. It was soon apparent that many of the principles of aerial archaeology, which were worked out in the early 20th century, are applicable in Jordan, but must be adapted to suit local conditions and local opportunities.

Sites of all periods and types might be located and photographed. In practice palaeolithic sites — which are abundant in Jordan, are virtually invisible from the air, but aerial photographs can help to set known early sites in their landscape context.

What we have achieved can now be set out and illustrated.

Aerial Archaeology in Jordan in the 21st Century

Finding

The JADIS database lists 8,680 'sites', a huge number, but that still represents only a third of the *c.* 25,000 found through interpretation of the 4,000 vertical photographs of western Jordan. The probability is that even the latter figure is no more than a quarter of those still surviving. The scope for 'finding' new sites is considerable. In two seasons we chose to explore the Jarash area with greater intensity and the following photographs illustrate the potential.

Figure 4.1 shows part of the site of Khirbat Ain. The several components to it include a tomb (Fig. 9.9C) and the structure shown here. Located on a ridge above the valley and the village, it had largely escaped attention (one reference being for a monastery on the hill-top), yet here in a single photograph one can see the clear outline of a small fort. A few kilometres to the west, an aerial view (Fig. 4.2) reveals two features not previously reported at all. The modern road skirts the edge of a rocky outcrop. In an earlier period, however, a road had run straight across the hillside and on the summit was built a small, square structure. Subsequent ground exploration revealed Roman pottery and traces of rock-cut shaft graves. The probability is that we are looking at a small Roman road-station on a hitherto unreported road southeast of Jarash.

Rather different are the traces to be seen in the Basalt Desert to the east. Figure 4.3 shows the bold outline of

Fig. 4.6. An ancient farm and fossilized fields near the Wadi el-Hasa (APA02.2/ SL23.3, 30 September 2002)

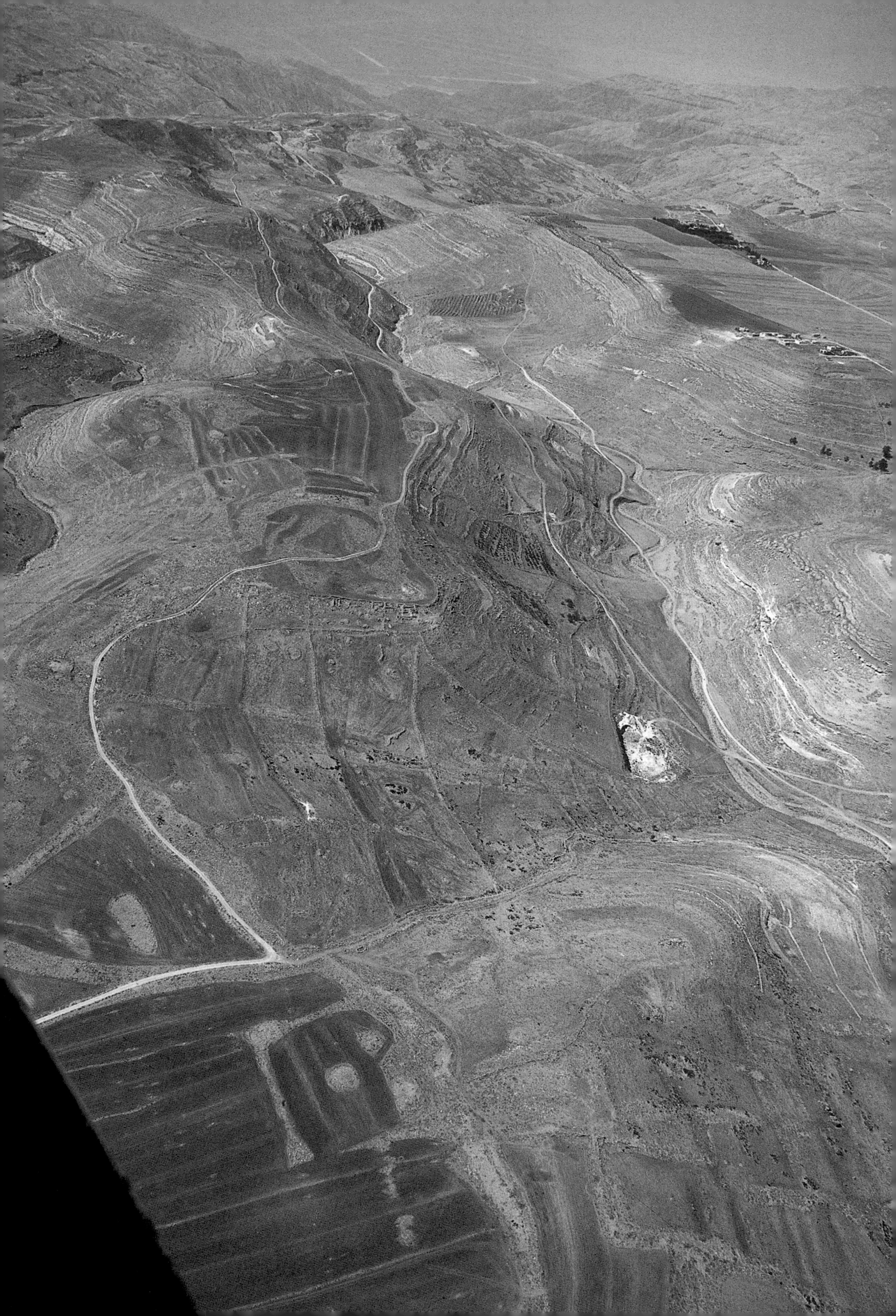

Fig. 4.7: On the hills between Damieh and Salt (APA98/ SL27.5, 17 May 1998)

a rectangular structure. It is plainly old and its walls have been partly re-used to create animal pens in more recent times. The site was in fact, first noted on an old vertical photograph. But as one can see in the background, the obvious structure is only a part of the overall complex. Showing as a very pale grey, that would be hard to notice or interpret at ground level, is a series of structures similar to the 'jellyfish' and 'wheel houses' discussed in Chapter 5 (Fig. 5.5).

Much further east is this example near Safawi (Fig. 4.4). At ground level the dark outline of small modern animals pens, which abound in the Basalt Desert, are clear enough, which is not the case for the large 'wheel house' just below right of centre. It seems to be partly silted over, though surviving as an above-ground structure; from the air it is more intelligible.

Some archaeological features become a functioning part of the modern landscape. The 'kite' shown in Fig. 4.5 (cf. Fig. 5.4) has survived in an area where clearance for agriculture has been extensive. However, it was evidently of use and its walls have survived as boundary walls.

Recording

Recording on the ground can be laborious even in the best of circumstances. Some features are so extensive that such mapping is impractical or not cost-effective. From the air the task can be much easier. One example concerns a network of ancient tracks, first identified by French archaeologists a decade ago near Jarash. On the ground they are hard to spot, because they usually consist of a cleared path with a narrow border of rocks on either side resulting from the clearance. Tracing the path is difficult and mapping harder still. As Fig. 6.9B shows, such tracks stand out superbly from the air and the task of mapping is relatively easy when armed with a suitable base map of the area.

In the same way, one can deal with any other type of structure, which is large or common. Chapter 5 illustrates examples of 'desert kites' (Figs 4.5 and 5.4). As explained there, these are hard to understand at ground level; they cover large areas and are very numerous. Air photographs offer an easy method of finding them, mapping them in a simple fashion and even providing rough sketch plans of each, to provide the basis for a comparative study.

Fig. 4.8: A farm and cross walls south of Umm el-Jimal (APA98/ SL9.25, 12 May 1998)

Fig. 4.9. Hibabiya and olive plantations in the Basalt Desert (APA02.1/ SL7.35, 2 April 2002)

With low-level oblique views and some fixed reference points on the ground, one can interpret and map these 'kites' in detail. Though less numerous, the same procedure may be applied to wheel houses.

In the south of Jordan, just north of the Wadi el-Hasa, one confronts extensive traces of fossilized fields. Too extensive to map easily on the ground and probably difficult to disentangle, the aerial view can provide the solution (Fig. 4.6). Just left of centre are the traces of ruined buildings. Beyond are enclosures associated with this probable farm; and further around still, are the grey banks of ancient stone clearance, marking the outlines of early fields.

The final example was encountered by chance while flying from the Jordan Valley to Salt (Fig. 4.7). There on the hillside was a series of earthworks: terraces, field boundaries and apparent tumuli. Not only was it found from the air, but it can be mapped from the aerial photographs.

Interpretation

The following chapters offer many instances of the aerial view as a guide to interpretation and understanding. Much more useful in many ways is the application applied to the far more numerous, but less visible sites, that have not made it to our list for illustrations. Figure 4.8 shows a simple farm south of Umm el-Jimal. The complex of buildings can be seen at ground level but is hard to decipher. From the air the form and something of the detail can be seen. More importantly, why it is there is clear: the vegetation in May reveals the wadi and the succession of cross walls built to impede the runoff in winter and create fields for cultivation.

Monitoring

Aerial reconnaissance is routinely used in Europe to monitor landscapes under threat, or vulnerable sites. Everywhere in Jordan is under threat in varying degrees, as two examples will illustrate. In the Hauran, close to the frontier with Syria, lies the beduin village of Umm al-Quttein. In 1976 it had a population of 201; in 1994 it was 3,064 with predictions of a five-fold increase for the wider area by 2013. Thirty kilometres to the south is the dusty series of mud pans called qas. They flood in winter rains and have a thin surface of water, which probably

Fig. 4.10. Khirbat Arbid (APA01/ SL11.7, 3 October 2001)

explains the numerous structures in the vicinity, of every period from prehistory onwards. Twenty years ago this area was largely deserted; today, using bulldozers to create dams and enclosures, and pumps to move the water harvested in winter, vast areas have been planted with olive trees (Fig. 4.9). This is a development that has happened within just a decade or so and almost unseen in this seemingly remote place. But it has swept away hundreds of ancient sites, the only record of which is preserved on old air photographs. Lost, without much trace, is the unique prehistoric village called Hibabiya which once lay on the basalt high ground in the centre of this photograph. A multi-disciplinary investigation project, with both research and salvage objectives, is required urgently before too much is lost.

Two further examples illustrate the need for a programme of aerial monitoring in Jordan. First is the series of walls and structures known as Khirbat Arbid, south of Lejjun (Fig. 4.10). It lies close to a major road and farming is spreading into the area. It is only a matter of time before it begins to be damaged: aerial reconnaissance can be employed; first to make a permanent record; second to help map the remains; and third to watch for developments and alert archaeologists to the danger.

Ma'an is a large town in southern Jordan, occupied for at least 2,000 years because of its springs. As we shall see in Chapter 14, the distinctive mud tower houses are disappearing fast, with little record being made (Fig. 14.9A). More startling, however, is what happened just recently a few kilometres to the east. Figure 4.11 is of a site called Hammam. It is one of three very similar sites in an area of ancient cultivation east of Ma'an. As the photograph shows it consists of a large ancient reservoir, ruins on either side, a large square *qasr* — a caravanserai or residence (centre) — and the outlines of fields. That was in May 1998. In September 2000, when the site was monitored again, the entire interior of the *qasr* had been bulldozed. In September 2002, a further flight was unable to detect where the *qasr* had been, as bulldozing had completed the job. In 2003 a further flight showed that bulldozing had been extended further to clear the area around where the *qasr* had once been.

Tourism

Finally there is culture heritage and tourism. The potential for Jordan for promoting its archaeological sites is immense. As the rest of this book sets out to illustrate, Jordan is richly strewn with wonderful sites of every period and kind, and often superbly preserved. There is scope for extensive exploitation of this cultural heritage which, if handled carefully and sensitively in collaboration with archaeologists, can serve the needs of academics and the nation. As noted above in relation to Britain, the income from selling heritage can be immense. And it is sustainable. However, it is not just that heritage has a monetary value; it is non-renewable, so every country should use its inheritance carefully and wisely. The cultural heritage of Jordan is very rich, well dispersed and, in places, well preserved, but it is also fragile and finite.

Conclusion

The history of aerial reconnaissance in the country, as outlined above, means that the photography and reconnaissance undertaken by the authors since 1997 is very much a beginning. In comparison with European countries — for example there has been almost one hundred years of aerial survey in the United Kingdom — there are still many years of reconnaissance to be done. Our work has literally only scratched the surface. Repeated, annual programmes of reconnaissance will produce many new discoveries, as well as increasing our understanding of the threats and changes to archaeological sites in the rapidly developing country.

Approximately 400 sites have been photographed since 1997 which is only 5% of the sites in the Jordanian Archaeological Database and Information System. This database in turn probably only represents a tenth of all archaeological sites in the country. Thus, there is still enormous scope for future archaeological aerial surveys in Jordan. Happily the Jordanian authorities have proved generous and far-sighted. A further programme of flying has been approved for 2004 and we hope this activity will continue for many years to come.

Fig. 4.11: Ma'an — Hammam (APA98/ SL18.32, 14 May 1998)

Fig. 5.1B: Beidha: the PPNB 'village' (APA02.2/ SL26.8, 30 September 2002)

Beidha

Tourists scarcely know of Beidha yet archaeologically it is one of the most significant sites in Jordan. It is also in a delightful location **(Fig. 5.1A)** and well worth the trip; it lies 5 km north from Wadi Musa, near Petra. Indeed, it can be combined with a visit to the Siq el-Barada — the so-called Cold Siq where some little-known but impressive Nabataean tombs lie at an alternative entrance to Petra.

The site lies in a rectangular bay in the mountain range, with a wadi flowing out along the southern edge (right); the settlement is on higher ground (partly man-made) beneath a towering bluff.

Excavations by Diana Kirkbride, spread over 8 seasons beginning in 1958, dug down through as much as 6 m of deposits, to reveal no less than 8 phases of occupation, extending over about 500 years. The buildings were remarkably well preserved after so many millennia. Each successive phase increased in complexity, which makes the place especially interesting for understanding the development of society and economy in the region. More than that however, is its very early date and the rarity of sites of this period.

Excavation revealed seasonal occupation of the 11th millennium BC, in what is known as the Natufian period. Remains included buildings, storage facilities, and hearths, as well as flint tools and animal bones. Much excitement was caused by the next period of settlement, 4,000 years later, when the first permanent Neolithic settlement appeared. Sites of the 7th millennium are rare and this Pre-Pottery Neolithic B (PPNB) site was not only uniquely well preserved, but also large enough to be characterized as a village, one of the earliest ever found.

Unlike the seasonal camps of the earlier Natufian period this settlement was continuous for 5 centuries. Architectural change occurred through time beginning with curvilinear buildings, which became progressively more densely packed, gradually changing until they were rectilinear in plan. Some may have been two storeys high and a few seem to have been community structures — perhaps for ritual or organizational purposes; in all 65 buildings were revealed.

As **Figure 5.1B** shows, the remains were largely left exposed and we can easily pick out the clusters of rooms and see examples of both shapes; on the right is the start of a recent modern reconstruction. The intention of the latter is to explore the possibilities as to how these circular buildings may have been roofed, to show tourists what parts of the site may have looked like and to provide a small visitor centre.

Unlike the modest quantities of Natufian period finds, the Neolithic (PPNB) village was rich in artefacts and floral and faunal remains. Renewed work on the charcoal has identified oak, juniper and pistachio as the favoured specifies for fuel for the fires.

Fig. 5.1A: Beidha: the valley and PPNB 'village' (APA00/ SL7.9 (RHB), 14 September 2000)

Fig. 5.2B: Basta (APA2002.2/ SL25.26, 30 September 2002)

Basta

Twenty kilometres south of Petra is a second important Pre-Pottery Neolithic B (7th millennium) settlement **(Fig. 5.2A).** Its remains first came to light only in 1972 through excavation, while survey of the area only began in 1984. The settlement grew up beside a spring and ultimately artefacts were distributed over a very wide area (24 ha). It seems, however, that occupation shifted over the area so that the size of the settlement at any one time was rather more limited. Excavation has been extensive with nearly 1 ha in total opened up across the site. The figure shows the modern village with a recent area of excavation at centre right.

The village contains rectangular buildings with multiple rooms; walls still survive to the height of the window frames. Rooms seem to cluster round courtyards and some may have been two-storeyed. A curiosity of the site is the network of channels, which seem to have allowed air circulation beneath the rooms. In places walls had traces of plaster, some of it decorated. **Figure 5.2B** shows a recent trench inside which can be seen a courtyard area, with rows of square rooms and elongated rectangular ones.

This was a complex society, as the abundant waste material attests, and skilled craftsmanship is represented by the quality of the artefacts. In the later phases stone vessels began to be paralleled by clay ones.

A further feature of the site is the usage of rooms for burials, a common enough practice, but a staggering three-quarters are children under 7 years. Examination of the skeletal remains has revealed a wide range of ailments, from arthritis to scurvy.

Fig. 5.2A: Basta — view looking south over the village (APA2002.2/ SL25.19, 30 September 2002)

Fig. 5.3B: Teleilat el-Ghassul: looking northeast (APA98/ SL28.11, 17 May 1998)

Teleilat el-Ghassul

The land between the junction of the Jordan River with the Dead Sea, and the hills rising steeply to the east, is flat and intensively farmed. The image **(Fig. 5.3A)** is a misleading one as to how this area looked *c.* 7,000 years ago. Then it was an area of marshland with sandbanks offering firm ground to would-be settlers. In the foreground of this photograph is the best known of these early settlements, Teleilat el-Ghassul, 6 km east of the Jordan and 5 km from the nearest corner of the Dead Sea.

The significance of the site has been known since the 1920s and it has been the object of extensive excavation by various teams and nationalities for half a century. The explanation lies in the discovery here of a Late Neolithic settlement which developed and flourished in the Chalcolithic period (*c.* 5700–3600 BC). Indeed, the site has come to be used as a defining term — Ghassulian — for this period on both sides of the Jordan River.

What excavators uncovered was an early agricultural community, which, at its greatest extent in this Chalcolithic period, lasted for the better part of a thousand years and may have extended over as much as 20–25 ha. Structures were circular in the Late Neolithic, but gave way in the Chalcolithic to long rectangular buildings of mud-brick. Unlike Basta and Beidha (cf. Figs 5.1 and 5.2), there was little internal division of such structures. On the other hand, walls were often not just plastered, but decorated with religious scenes of people and buildings. One part of the site, with two large rectangular buildings, was divided off for what appears to have been religious purposes.

Fig. 5.3B shows the site in more detail. Clearest, are the long fingers of the excavators spoil heaps leading away from the trenches themselves. Here and there can be seen the traces of building forms.

Fig. 5.3A: Teleilat el-Ghassul: panorama looking northeast (APA98/ SL28.12, 17 May 1998)

Fig. 5.4A: Kite in Jebel Qatafi (APA98/ 32.33, 18 May 1998)

Fig. 5.4B: Kite north of the Azraq Oasis (APA02.1/ 6.18, 1 April 2002)

Fig. 5.4C: Linked kites and a wheel house on Jebel Aseikhim (APA02.1/ 6.31, 1 April 2002)

Desert Kites

The so-called 'kite sites' are amongst the commonest type of archaeological site in Jordan. They are enigmatic and surprisingly varied. At ground level they are often only visible when one is standing close to, or on part of, the structure. Not so from the air. From above they stand out clearly and offer the only serious means of understanding their pattern and mapping them. One has only to consider their numbers (1,000s) and scale (100 m upwards) to understand the problems and possible solutions when trying to quantify and analyse their distribution (Ch. 4).

The RAF pilots who were establishing the airmail route from Cairo to Baghdad in the 1920s first applied the name 'kite'. Impressed by the number, size and shape of these stone-built structures, they were reminded of a kite: the long walls being the string and the tail, and the enclosure being the body of the kite.

Size varies. The heads can range from 50 to 100+ m in diameter and tails commonly run out for a 100 m, sometimes several hundred metres and occasionally over a kilometre. The head is an enclosure but it can be curvilinear or angular with points to create a crude star shape. The enclosure has a narrow opening where the tails join it.

Kites are generally set out with the tails opening along the bottom of a slope and converging before entering the head, which lies over the crest out of sight. They are commonly in groups, indeed, in parallel chains, whose tails often overlap or can even be joined.

Despite past exotic proposals there seems no serious doubt that they were animal traps. The Arabic name, in the singular *masyada*, means hunting trap or net and they were for trapping antelope, gazelle and ostrich, which abounded in this region until the arrival of hunters with guns and motorized vehicles. There is evidence of migrating herds of gazelle, and the broad distribution of these hunting grounds may support the concept of the hunter and the hunted moving together.

Although one of the most numerous archaeological site types in the Middle East they are one of the least studied. They represent a huge undertaking, imply considerable organization and suggest a more varied economy than might have been expected in such a seemingly barren area.

In the first example **(Fig. 5.4A)**, in Jebel Qatafi 150 km east of the Azraq Oasis, gazelle would be driven towards the widely splayed tails on the centre left and funnelled towards the head on the centre right. As in other examples, the tails continue well into the head, so that panic-stricken animals inside would find it hard to rediscover the opening. Several 'hides' for hunters are visible around the perimeter of the head.

Figure 5.4B is north of Azraq, but in an area with a basalt background, which makes kites harder to see at ground level. Here tails begin in the distance and almost converge after entering the head. The head is a star shape again and the small circular hides on the 'points' are very clear.

The two final examples **(Fig. 5.4C)** are again just north of Azraq on the northern slope of Jebel Aseikhim. The 'body' at the top left is over 200 m across; four long 'tails' and at least two shorter ones, running back towards the viewer, are hundreds of metres long (cf. the nomad tents and truck in the foreground). But note how the tail on the right loops back upwards to form the tail of the second kite on the right. Animals driven towards these kites would be bound to enter one.

In the example on the left, a tail has been overlain later by another common desert structure, a wheel house.

Fig. 5.5A: A wheel and jellyfish house village (APA98/ SL33.30, 18 May 1998)

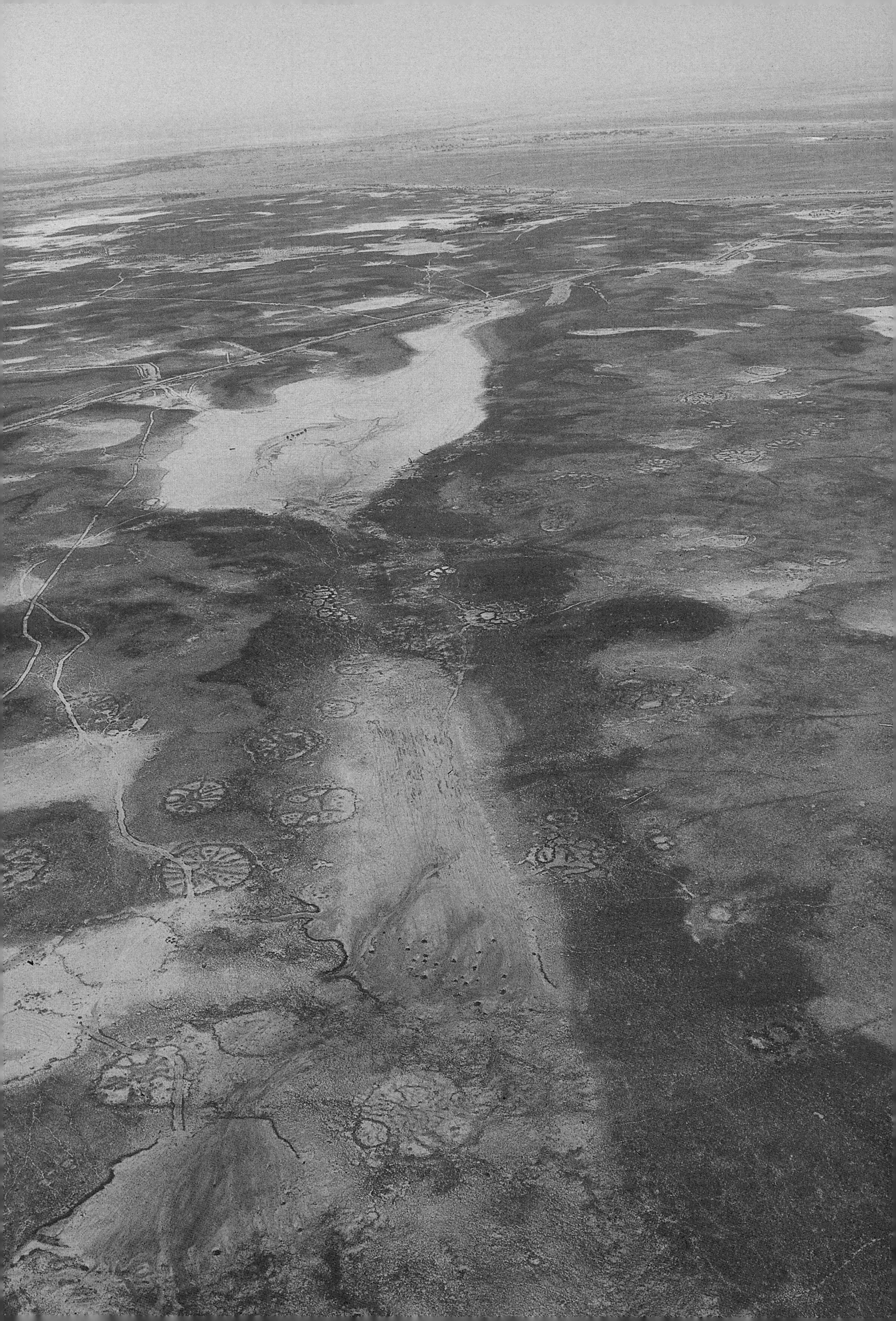

Fig. 5.5C: A wheel house (APA98/ SL31.20, 18 May 1998)

Wheel and Jellyfish Houses

Prehistoric houses like this **(Fig. 5.5A)** are scattered in the hundreds across the Basalt Desert of northeastern Jordan (cf. Fig. 4.4).

In the boulder-strewn landscape stretching northeast from Amman structures abound, but are hard to detect at ground level. Even when found they are difficult to envisage and interpret. This low oblique view of one group, 5 km southwest of the oasis of Azraq Duruz, is a superb example of the two main types.

In this group are 29 circular huts, including several wheels. It might almost be called a village. Many are found close to the areas of mud flat on which water ponded in winter and could be retained longer by digging pits. Certainly the same locations remain popular with modern beduin, whose camps and animal pens are often beside, or even reusing, the ancient sites.

There are variants in form, ranging from those with walls radiating from the centre to a rim (wheel), to others that are a collection of irregular enclosures inside a circle (jellyfish). In the foreground of this view **(Fig. 5.5B)** we can see a modified wheel house, *c.* 50 m in diameter, around the exterior of which is a ring of small circular huts, *c.* 4–5 m in diameter. Sometimes these rings of huts are found without the inner wheel house. Three more wheel houses extend beyond, but even from above, this oblique angle already makes the last one hard to see.

The third view **(Fig. 5.5C)** is a superb example complete, in this case, with central 'hub' and well-defined external hut circles.

In some places wheel houses are found beside, or even overlying, parts of kites implying the latter are contemporary or older. In **Figure 5.4C** we saw an example where the hut had caused stones to be removed from the kite tail, implying the latter is older. Flints have been found at many of these huts, but so too has some coarse pottery. From the little research done on them, the suggestion has arisen that they may represent the regularly visited seasonal camping grounds of nomads, perhaps extending from as far back as the 6th millennium BC. Function too is uncertain. Walls are low — now less than a metre — and may have been animal pens. The hut rings may be the foundations of houses with a temporary awning for roofing.

Fig. 5.5B: Wheel houses (APA97/ SL5.17, 27 May 1997)

Fig. 5.6A: A double-walled enclosure or chain site (APA02.1/ SL4.35, 1 April 2002)

Hut circle enclosures, Walls and Stone Heaps

The Basalt Desert is strewn with enigmatic structures, few of which have been studied in detail, so that little can be said about their date or purpose. At one of the sites — a hut circle near **Figure 5.6A**, but of the kind seen best in **Figure 5.6B** — flint artefacts were noted of a type dated variously to the PPNB Late Neolithic and even Late Chalcolithic. But such dating is insecure and many features may be more recent.

A type of site encountered at several places around the Azraq Basin is the double-walled enclosure illustrated in **Figure 5.6A.** In this example *c.* 1,500 m southwest of the fort at Azraq Duruz (Fig. 13.5), the outline shows sharply against the pale yellow of an area of mudflat. As the car track across the top of the photograph shows, the site is large, *c.* 70 x 45 m. As with others nearby, the outer enclosure wall forms a C shape, all of which open to the east. The 'walls' are of basalt boulders and are up to 10 m wide in places. That represents the collapse however, and in places there are traces of circular hollows inside the wall, implying it was a chain of rooms, rather than a solid wall. In practice, this type of site may be the same as one of the site types seen in the next photograph.

Fig. 5.6B: Hut circle enclosures, walls and cairns near Qasr Uweinid (APA02.1/ SL3.19, 1 April 2002)

In **Figure 5.6B** we are looking at the plateau running north from the small Roman and Islamic fort of Qasr Uweinid, *c.* 14 km southwest of Azraq Duruz. In contrast to the landscape to the south and below the fort, which is largely devoid of visible sites, the basalt plateau is an incredible tangle of circles, huts, kites and 'walls'. Despite a few modern tracks cutting the area, we can still see an extraordinary mix of structures of all kinds on the surface and hints of buried features too. Just left of centre is a kite with one tail running towards each of the bottom corners of the photograph. All around, however, are hut circles — structures consisting of small circular huts arranged in a circle. Sometimes there are other features inside the ring; sometimes they are empty. In the 1920s an RAF observer of this group counted 11 examples. Then there are also dozens of inexplicable stretches of wall and scores of cairns.

About 20 km north of Azraq Duruz is one of a number of areas marked by a scatter of large cairns **(Fig. 5.6C).** In this example, about 100 cairns are visible, each 2–4 m in diameter (compare the track width). Most are on the east side of a wadi (which still has pools of water in April) most too, are randomly scattered, though, just left of centre one group seems to form a circle. Here and there tiny yellow dots on the centres suggest they may originally have been open inside or have been robbed in the middle. There is much more to be seen in the photograph — other walls, structures and modern corrals, a common feature of the Basalt Desert.

6. THE BRONZE AGE

The Bronze Age is well represented in the archaeological record both from excavation and extensive ground survey. Sites are numerous and found widely across the country. The difficulty from the present perspective is in *seeing* Bronze Age features: as significant Bronze Age settlements were occupied, or re-occupied in the Iron Age and in later periods too. In illustrating Bronze Age sites what one often sees in the photograph are the traces of these later phases. What is being illustrated here, therefore, is sometimes the chosen location and something of the scale and nature of the site, rather than the details of Bronze Age structures and features.

Surveys repeatedly show a remarkable surge in the numbers of sites between the Early Bronze I and Early Bronze II (3600–2750 BC). Indeed, before modern times, only the Roman period has more sites. Along the Wadi Zarqa, for example, the fertile valley and perennial stream attracted numerous settlements on hilltops and promontories all the way from the citadel in Amman to the confluence with the River Jordan. Fortifications surround most of them and they are often in sight of one another. In the Jordan Valley it is the great mounds on the floodplain that catch the eye with, in many cases, the Iron Age or later phase overlying and obscuring a Bronze Age forerunner.

If the Bronze Age remains are not always visible, the location of the sites is clear. More than that, many of these choices by Bronze Age populations were to be of enduring importance — not just in the Iron Age but in later periods too. The Graeco-Roman city of Pella (Fig. 9.5) has very important Bronze Age levels, while the Bronze Age underlies almost all the other cities of the Roman Decapolis.

The Bronze Age is prominent much more widely than just in the fertile valleys and on the rich soils of the highlands. One of the best-known urban settlements is the 12 ha town and cemetery of Bab edh-Dhraʿ in the Lisan peninsula. Survey in the Hauran, along the Syrian frontier, has revealed scores of Bronze Age sites (Fig. 6.2), many of them paralleled or overlain by Roman and early Islamic successors. This was plainly a period of wide settlement, including into marginal areas. What made it possible was the growing sophistication in water management and storage, the development of which reached a peak in the Nabataean to early Islamic periods. Symbolic of this aspect of Bronze Age settlement in Jordan is the site with which we begin, Jawa, described by its excavator as 'the best preserved fourth millennium town yet discovered in the world', but unique in its location.

What is striking about the physical remains, too, is the character. There *are* urban settlements but most sites are more modest villages or farms. The suggestion has been made that the society was egalitarian, with few of the elites whose competitiveness in other periods drove development and change and nurtured cities.

Finally, a characteristic structure of the archaeology of the period is the dolmen, stone (slab) built tombs, very familiar as part of the megalithic tradition in western Europe. In Jordan, we have not just scattered examples, but entire cemeteries strewn extensively over hillsides.

Fig. 5.6C: Large cairns (APA02.1/ SL8.24, 2 April 2002)

Fig. 6.1B: Jawa (APA98/ SL8.28, 12 May 1998)

Jawa

This hilltop settlement is not, as was first thought, a Roman military installation. It is something far more remarkable — a fourth millennium BC urban centre set in the Basalt Desert of northeast Jordan.

This desert region of northeastern Jordan is unsuited for large-scale settlements at any time. Nomads, however, could and did exploit the limited resources of this area: they have been traced there as far back as at least 8,000 BC. Then, startlingly, just over 5,000 years ago, a large and sophisticated town appeared. As the photograph shows **(Fig. 6.1A)**, the outlines of both the massive Upper Town walls and those of the Lower Town are easily visible; so too, are houses and some of the public buildings excavated in the 1970s.

It was built as a planned and organized development (and not just an agglomeration of houses). Indeed, not only was the town 'planned' but its infrastructure of water and irrigation systems, reservoirs and storage systems, was also constructed in this early phase. At its fullest development, at the end of the 4th millennium BC, it was about 10 ha in area, with a population of perhaps 2,500–3,700 people sheltering inside an Upper Town, with walls *c.* 1 km long, and others inside the Lower Town, whose walls were longer still.

Excavation has revealed evidence for agriculture — farming tools, cereals, chickpea, lentil and even grape seeds. What sustained it all was a sophisticated understanding of water harvesting and control. The town is built above the Wadi Rajil and could exploit a catchment area of *c.* 300 sq km, stretching 35 km upstream. Dams, deflection dams, canals and reservoirs all helped provide large quantities of water for people, animals and irrigation farming. The rebuilt pools of today **(Fig. 6.1B)**, show how water can still easily be preserved from distant winter rains.

Why it occurred is unknown — population expansion from the west, where larger settlements (villages) were expanding into towns? Or was it a development of local population growth amongst the nomads? Whatever the explanation, the town did not survive long. The demand for water and possibly the initial success of the town, created the conditions for its own downfall.

There is archaeological evidence for definite and permanent breaches to the substantial defensive walls, not long after they had been constructed. The excavator inferred from this a violent seizure of the place, perhaps by nomads demanding access to its water collections. Subsequent rebuilding is indicative of a less well planned, more piecemeal development, in the Early and Middle Bronze Ages. The preservation of the Middle Bronze Age houses is very good, even to the extent of a roof surviving, held up by cantilevered basalt blocks.

The state of preservation raises many questions about the complete abandonment of the site, as successive generations have left the remains untouched and not used the stones for building their own houses. Since the Bronze Age the area has reverted to a survival system based on a nomadic way of life, relying on domesticated sheep and goats and whatever natural resources were available.

The excavations at Jawa have been immensely important in trying to understand the human use of this arid, inhospitable landscape. They have also helped to date the 'kite' sites (Fig. 5.4), many of which occur in this area and whose construction has been shown to pre-date Jawa's town building phase during the fourth millennium.

Fig. 6.1A: Jawa (APA98/ SL8.38, 12 May 1998)

Fig. 6.2B: Hauran sites (APA98/ SL8.4, 12 May 1998)

Bronze Age Hauran

The fertile lands of the Hauran straddling the modern border with Syria, are strewn with sites. Jawa lies just beyond the eastern edge of the area. As always, the 'Roman' period is dominant, but once again the Bronze Age is well represented. Ground survey in the Jordanian Hauran east of the small Roman town of Umm el-Jimal (Fig. 11.3), revealed dozens of sites with Bronze Age pottery. It is easy to see why — this is a fertile region with adequate rainfall for dry farming **(Fig. 6.2A**; cf. 2.10). Sites are often still very clear as areas of grey boulders and thick scatters of pottery and in many places quite substantial settlements were often just a few hundred yards apart. In this view there is a site beneath the modern village. A second can be seen further away along the track while a third is to the right and further away again. Few have names and most are known only from the collection of ancient pottery sherds.

Figure 6.2B is a detail of the larger site in the previous view. It extends over an area of *c.* 200 x 200 m. The reservoir is again in use and the land all around is once more under intensive arable farming. Sherds are of various periods, but the Bronze Age is well represented.

Fig. 6.2A: Hauran sites (APA98/ SL8.3, 12 May 1998)

Fig. 6.3B: Lehun (APA98/ SL35.8, 20 May 1998)

Lehun

This is a site remarkable for its location, its extent, and its settlement in successive periods. The site lies on the north rim of the great slash of the Wadi Mujib, which runs down to the Dead Sea (right) (Fig. 2.3). This shallow, oblique view, illustrates the location of the site in a way not feasible at ground level. The eye is caught by the lozenge shape, where excavation trenches can be seen, but that is just one part of the site. It covers an area of 22.5 ha, the Nabataean, Roman, Mamluk and Ottoman being out of sight, below the left corner of the photograph. In fact, the site has traces from early prehistory to the small modern village, the periods of particular interest though are the Bronze Age and early Iron Age.

The Early Bronze Age (EBA) settlement is represented by the earthworks on the left in **Figure 6.3A** and at the top of **Figure 6.3B**. It began as an EBA I settlement, which was then replaced by a fortified town of EB II–III covering about 6 ha. A massive wall, 5–5.5 m wide, surrounded it, the west side of which, 270 m long, can be seen in both photographs as an earthwork overlooking the little Wadi Lehun which runs into the Wadi Mujib.

Small rectangular houses were excavated, some only of a single room, some with their own cisterns. Elsewhere, there were olive presses, a street and two large reservoirs with a capacity of *c.* 1,200 cu m, the depressions for which can be seen in **Figure 6.3B**. The olive presses, animal bones and the presence of rich arable land to the north leave little doubt this was a thriving agricultural and pastoral community.

After a hiatus in the Late Bronze Age (*c.* 1,300 BC) major settlement re-appeared, but shifted now to the southwest, to the area appearing as a large lozenge and where most excavation has centred. Three features stand out in the photographs. First the long circuit wall enclosing the *c.* 6,500 sq m of this new town and showing as a casemate wall — two parallel walls, with cross walls, to form rooms in its thickness. Second is the scatter of rectilinear houses, this time augmented by evidence for storage buildings, grain mills and weaving. Calculations have suggested about 80–100 houses and an overall population of perhaps, 500–1,000 people.

The third feature is the Iron Age II fort at the southernmost point, where it overlooks the wadi below. It is 37 x 43 m and has casemate walls and a central courtyard. There are four internal corner towers, unique in central Jordan, probably because there was not enough room for construction on the steep cliff outside. Breaches in the defence show that the fort was attacked and presumably later abandoned. This is one of a number of Iron Age forts built in this area; other examples will be looked at in the next chapter. It is now, too, that evidence of contact with Egypt is provided by a faience scarab of the XXth dynasty (1186–1070 BC); shortly after this period the site was abandoned once more.

Fig. 6.3A: Lehun (APA98/ SL35.2, 20 May 1998)

Fig. 6.4B: Khirbat ez-Zeraqun (APA2002.2/ SL16.11, 29 September 2002)

Khirbat ez-Zeraqun

This Early Bronze Age site occupies one of the most attractive locations in Jordan. About 11 km northeast of Irbid and overlooking from the west side, a loop of the Wadi ash-Shallalah **(Fig. 6.4A)**. In this view, Zeraqun is one of three sites running across the view, at the point represented by a line a quarter of the way down from the top. Zeraqun in on the high ground on the right. Just visible, in the middle to its left, is the very pale white hill of Tell el-Fukhar (mainly EBA through to LBA). Towards the top left, is Tell Sabba (Chalcolithic and Iron II to Persian) on an almost conical hill, in a bay of the wadi, thickly planted with olive trees. The Roman bridge discussed elsewhere (cf. Fig. 9.10B) is in the wadi just beyond Zeraqun

The site is large — *c.* 400 x 300 m, one of the largest EBA sites in Jordan and neighbouring Syria. As at Lehun **(Fig. 6.3)**, the EBA I phase is found under the walls of the later major EBA II–III phases. In **Figure 6.4B** we can see the site crowning the hilltop with the two main areas of recent excavation. In both areas there is evidence of the massive city wall and the line of it can be seen in the photograph curving between the two areas. It is *c.* 7 m thick with projecting towers and bastions. On the highest point (the excavations on the right) there is not only the wall but also, an apparent gateway, the traces of a stone temple with a circular platform identified as the base of an altar and an administration building. Evidently this was the upper town or acropolis. In the lower town area (left), there are rectangular domestic buildings and the remains of a main street and small connecting ones.

Water could be obtained from the nearby spring but the site also boasted three shafts, one of them about 100 m deep, cutting down to the watertable in the wadi: a remarkable piece of hydraulic engineering.

Fig. 6.4A: Khirbat ez-Zeraqun (APA2002.2/ SL16.16, 29 September 2002)

Fig. 6.5B: Iktanu (APA98/ 28.16, 17 May 1998)

Iktanu

This is one of the most significant tell sites in the Jordan valley. It lies on the eastern edge of the Jordan Valley and 12 km northeast of the Dead Sea. Water and good soils attracted early farmers and explain the major Bronze Age site that developed into the tell shown here, at a nodal point of routes and resources **(Fig. 6.5A)**. The site is in two parts, divided into a North and a South Tell by the modern highway. The North Tell, surmounted by an Iron Age fort, is out of sight in this photograph. The South Tell, illustrated here, is the part with Bronze Age remains. The site has been seriously damaged in much more recent times by 20th century military trenches, then by bulldozing, both visible in this view.

Excavation has revealed evidence of an Early Bronze I settlement, a gap, then a major village site of the EB IV period. It covers a large area of *c.* 22 ha and is estimated to have had a population of 2,000–2,500 people. The structures themselves are visible in **Figure 6.5B** — stone built, rectangular rooms facing onto a courtyard and lanes between houses. Diet is inferred from remains recovered at the site, which point to arable farming, stock raising and hunting.

Fig. 6.5A: Iktanu (APA98/ 28.14, 17 May 1998)

Fig. 6.6B: Tell el-Husn (APA98/ SL21.10, 16 May 1998)

Tell el-Husn

This imposing site lies about 8 km south of Irbid at a place where the wadi systems drained off on either side towards the Yarmuk in the north and the Jordan valley to the west. **Figure 6.6A** shows the attraction of the site for the settlers whose successive layers of occupation debris created the mound: the fertile plain that surrounds it, which was as ideal in the past as it is now, for the cultivation of cereal crops.

It was described half a century ago by the American archaeologist Nelson Glueck as lifting itself 'commandingly and ponderously above the surrounding plain'. Despite the growth of the modern town, the tell, or mound, is still prominent and in spring the vegetation offers a striking contrast between the green of the mound, the white houses and the rich soils.

Settlement has probably been continuous here for almost four millennia resulting in a tall flat-topped hill built up over a natural outcrop. The dimensions are *c.* 180 x 275 m. The mound certainly goes back to at least the Bronze Age and there are sherds of all the EBA phases. But there are also significant traces of occupation from the Iron Age, Roman, Early Islamic and medieval Arab periods. Among the modern houses below the mound are remains of Roman occupation, including graves and tombs. This is one of the locations suggested for the Roman town of Dium, which lay somewhere in this part of northwestern Jordan, but whose location has never been determined. On the summit of the mound **(Fig. 6.6B)** are remains of ruined buildings and the outline of two sides of a fortification wall. The white speckles on the surface are a modern cemetery.

Fig. 6.6A: Tell el-Husn (APA98/ SL21.7, 16 May 1998)

Fig. 7.1B: Deir Alla (APA98/ SL26.24, 17 May 1998)

Deir Alla

The tell lies 4 km north of where the Wadi Zarqa comes down out of the hills into the Jordan Valley. On the flat irrigated lands of the Valley, the ancient site stands out clearly **(Fig. 7.1A).**

It is a large tell about 200 m in diameter and towering above the modern road and village. As the views show, it has been under excavation for many years, but only a small part has yet been revealed. Several periods are represented but the main evidence is for the Iron Age occupation.

As a tell of this scale implies, Deir Alla was a place of some significance. Some scholars think it may have been the Sukkoth of the Old Testament which was certainly important.

Excavation has revealed a major settlement on the site in the Chalcolithic and Late Bronze Age. The latter included extensive evidence of metalworking and included the first of a number of important written texts from the site. It ended in destruction in the 12th century BC. The major phase known from archaeology is the Iron Age II period (9th and 8th centuries in particular). In that period it was a substantial walled town within which have been found the traces of buildings with evidence for weaving and cult practices. The latter seem especially important, implying a 'high place' and, combined with textual sources, a pantheon for a variety of gods. The supposition is that, as in the Bronze Age, the strategically important location on a route between Egypt, the Levant and Mesopotamia, made it an important stopping place and culturally mixed. It is from this Iron Age II period that several early Aramaic inscriptions of *c.* 800 BC have come.

Figure 7.1B was taken in low slanting light, which highlights the scale of the mound and the depth of the trenches as revealed by the deep shadows. Work has continued and there is now (2002) a visitor centre in the corner nearest the camera with a staircase in place up to the top of the tell. The trench on the summit (right of centre) is a modern military installation.

Fig. 7.1A: Deir Alla: looking north-northwest (APA98/ SL26.18, 17 May 1998)

Fig. 7.2B: Dibon from the southeast (APA98/ SL34.35, 20 May 1998)

Dibon

Modern Dhiban lies in the far west of the Moabite plateau, on the ancient King's Highway *c.* 24 km south of Madaba and just 3 km before the highway plunges down into the great slash of the Wadi Mujib (Fig. 2.3). The tell itself is protected on the north, west and southwest by deep wadis. As the view shows **(Fig. 7.2A)**, there is a modern village on the southeast of the main tell. In the distance is part of the fertile plain.

Excavation has revealed occupation in the Early Bronze Age and — with gaps — many other later periods, most notably the Nabataean to early Umayyad, with the Roman, as always, prominent. The site is most famous, however, for its Iron Age remains. Two elements are prominent: first, in the 9th century BC it was the massively fortified capital of the Moabite kingdom and second it was the find-spot in 1868 of the famous stele of King Mesha, apparently set up on the tell site just northwest of the modern village. The Mesha Stone is still one of the most-important texts from this period for either side of the Jordan. King Mesha records — in a language very similar to Hebrew — his great achievements, not least his building work at Dibon, where he seems to have focussed on the creation of a royal quarter of the town. This work includes the sanctuary in which the stone was erected and which may, therefore, have been on the southeast side where the stone was found. Mesha also refers to construction in the royal quarter of walls, towers, gates, a palace, a reservoir and cistern.

The photographs show the scale of the mound against the buildings of the village and the road. Indeed, the village overlies what is a part of the ancient site, connected to the main tell by a low saddle: traces of ruins are still visible amongst the modern houses. Even in the distant view what strikes the eye is the massive wall and its substructures on the southeast side (cf. their scale — top left — against the adjacent modern house). The wall stands about 10 m high still and has been compared with the similarly massive work of King David at Jerusalem. Further stretches of wall have been uncovered, as well as a major Nabataean temple, a Roman (?) tower and a late Roman church. In the near-vertical view **(Fig. 7.2B),** looking south, the outlines of numerous other structures are visible beneath the soil and on the far right there may be the traces of a casemate wall running above the wadi.

Fig. 7.2A: Dibon from the southeast (APA98/ SL34.33, 20 May 1998)

Fig. 7.3B: Ed-Deir (APA98/ SL36.17, 20 May 1998)

Ed-Deir

The hilltop ruins of Ed-Deir **(Fig. 7.3A)** are located on the junction of the Kerak plateau and the steeply sloping cliffs overlooking the Dead Sea, about 7 km north-northwest of Kerak. It is strategically located on the summit of a ridge, linked by a narrow neck of land to the adjacent hills on the south. The site is over 1,000 m above sea level, with extensive views west down over the Dead Sea far below.

It is no surprise to find that this site has had a long period of occupation, spanning over 4,000 years, although probably not continuously occupied. There have only been surface surveys and excavation will be required to answer detailed questions. Some periods are well represented in the pottery record: the Iron Age, Nabataean–Roman and Islamic. Some scholars identify it with the Horonaim of the Hebrew Bible and the Mesha inscription.

The ruins cover an irregular area of 150 m x 165 m. There is a perimeter wall and a scatter of internal rectangular buildings. Many are quite well preserved as the detailed view shows **(Fig. 7.3B)**. Those visible are probably quite recent in date, but traces of earlier ones beneath are visible in places. Particularly striking is the large rectangular building in the centre on the highest point.

Fig. 7.3A: Ed-Deir (APA98/ SL36.15, 20 May 1998)

Fig. 7.4B: Rumeil (APA98/SL34.15, 20 May 1998)

Rumeil

On a plateau overlooking a broad valley to the north, about 17 km south-southeast of Madaba, lies one of the most unusual of the Moabite border fortresses. It is on the line of an ancient north–south route, which at this point has reached a ridge with a vista over the cereal fields all around **(Fig. 7.4A).** El-Mudayna (Fig. 7.7) is 3 km to the northeast and Kh. al-Heri (Fig. 7.6B) just beyond that.

The site resembles a wheel — a powerful central hub, traces of spokes and a rim. Closer inspection shows that it is in fact flattened on the northern side, where it runs up to the edge of the ridge. The diameter is about 115 m, with a width of about 70 m **(Fig. 7.4B).**

In the centre is the massive bulk of a tall square tower *c.* 16 x 9 m. Next come a mass of stone buildings which pack the interior up to the rampart and hub. The main entrance seems to have been on the northeast side. Deep shadows show how high the surrounding wall still stands above the rock-cut ditch which encircles it. Other buildings underlie the earthworks outside the circuit wall and there are cisterns all around.

The pottery implies a limited period of occupation and discounts older notions that it was a Roman military site.

Fig. 7.4A: Rumeil (APA98/SL34.13, 20 May 1998)

Fig. 7.5A: Khirbat Mdeinet Aliya (APA01/SL16.16, 5 October 2001)

Khirbat Mdeinet Aliya

In this dramatic view **(Fig. 7.5A),** the outline of the fortress and some internal buildings at Khirbat Mdeinet Aliya can be seen on a promontory of the great Wadi Mujib just where it joins the Wadi Lejjun. (Lejjun itself, including its large Bronze Age site, lies *c.* 5 km to the south-southwest.) The name, Mdeinet Aliya, means 'city' and is one of several in the vicinity with this element in the name, including one very similar to this just a few kilometres away on the same side of the Mujib. In fact, the rims of the Mujib and its tributaries are marked by a succession of sites, ranging from major settlements like this one, to towers. In this case, it seems to have been largely overlooked despite its extent, and only two academic commentators mention it in the entire 20th century.

There is a spring in the wadi below, but as the photograph underlines, this is a location chosen not for its access to farmland, but for its natural defensibility. The promontory is linked to the plateau by a narrow land bridge, which was strengthened by the trench visible in the panoramic view and then by the tower, whose ruins are just to its right. The enclosed area measures 275 x 110 m at its broadest and consists of a double wall running round the perimeter of the promontory. The walls themselves are often of very large blocks and the entire circuit stands out clearly **(Fig. 7.5B).** Many buildings can be seen inside, mainly constructed against this perimeter wall.

Erosion has carried away artefacts from both the interior and the slopes outside; the few collected are Bronze and Iron Age and the probability is that the fortress is primarily an Iron Age site.

Fig. 7.5B: Khirbat Mdeinet Aliya (APA01/SL16.13, 5 October 2001)

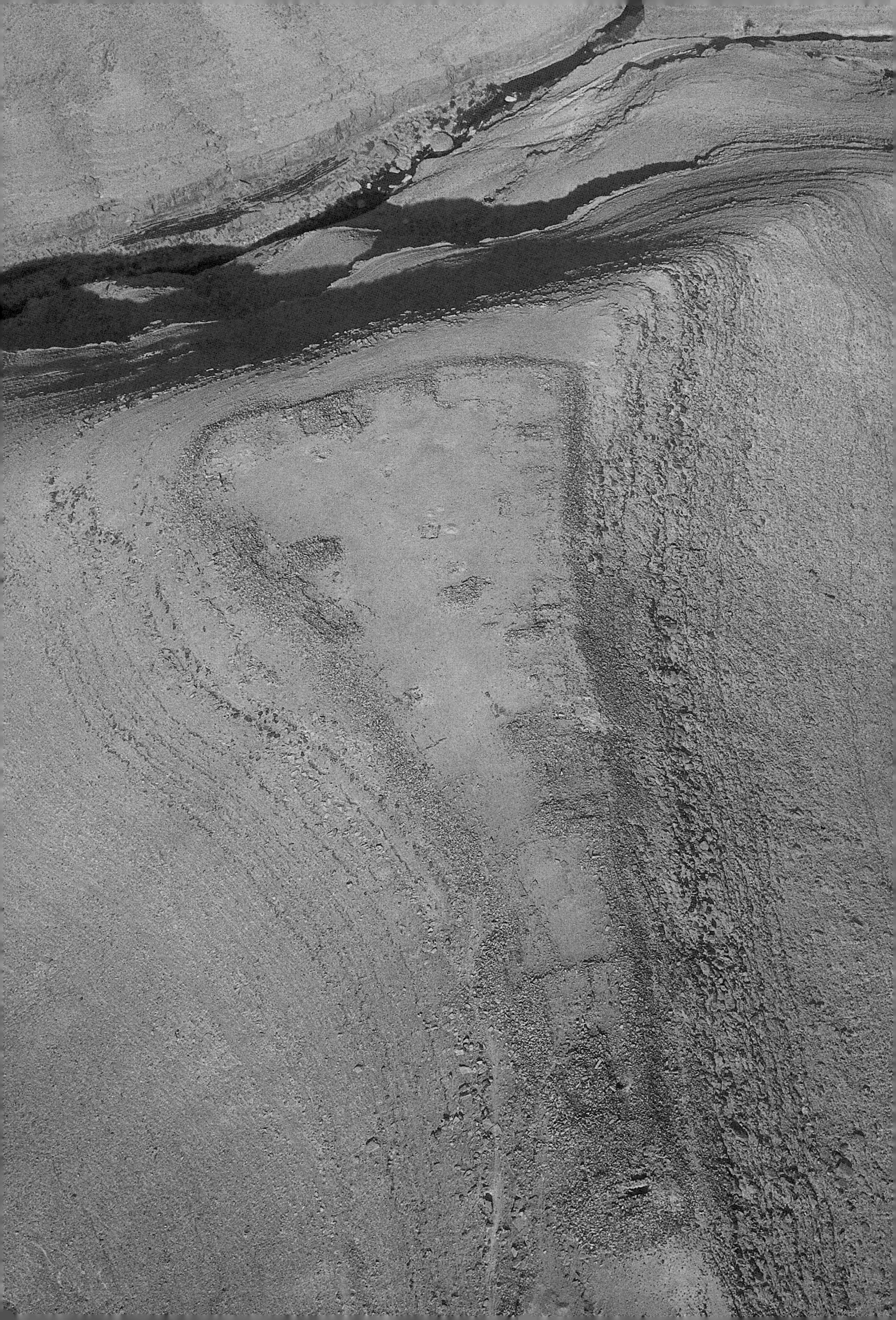

Fig. 7.6B: Khirbat al-Heri (APA98/ SL12.6, 13 May 1998)

Meidan and Khirbat al-Heri

Although both of the Moabite forts illustrated here are in similar specular and commanding positions, they are rather different in character.

Meidan, *c.* 20 km southwest of Kerak has three main elements. One part lies at the far end of the ploughed field in the centre of the view **(Fig. 7.6A)** and is probably Nabataean. Just right of centre is a small square structure seldom noted by visitors. Finally the Iron Age remains are on the promontory in the foreground. They consist of a curving wall, showing grey here, 1.25 m thick and *c.* 23 m in diameter. On the left side is an apparent inner 'blockhouse'. As the photograph shows, the site has a view northwest to the Lisan peninsula, as well as over the southern parts of the Dead Sea.

Khirbat al-Heri is a well-preserved example of a Moabite fort **(Fig. 7.6B).** Its location on a commanding peak, visible from a distance on all sides, was probably designed to watch over the fertile lands to the west and south and as an outpost for the impressive Iron Age settlement of Kh. el-Mudayna, in the Wadi ath-Thamad below (Fig. 7.7). It is a large rectangular fort, some 75 x 50 m, still standing two metres high. The interior is a baffling jumble of fallen masonry, but the view shows how even today it is an enormously impressive site.

Illicit digging has left pitting on the slopes amongst the remains of cisterns for rain water. In the further distance in Figure 7.6B can be seen the traces of buildings of what is thought to be a Roman settlement, described by Buckingham, the travelling antiquarian, as long ago as 1816 as 'a ruined town'.

Fig. 7.6A: Meidan (APA98/ SL36.32, 20 May 1998)

Fig. 7.7B: Khirbat el-Mudayna (APA98/ SL34.18, 20 May 1998)

Khirbat el-Mudayna

Figure 7.7A shows the 'city' (*medina*) *c.* 500 m from and on the south side of the Wadi ath-Thamad. The dense green vegetation of the wadi and the standing water, still there in late May 1998, help explain the attractions of the place. There are numerous other Iron Age sites in the vicinity, not least Kh. al-Heri on the peak to the north (Fig. 7.6B) and Rumeil to the southwest (Fig. 7.4).

The site dominates the valley as a long, narrow mound, the deep shadows accentuating the circuit walls. The recent excavations (since 1996) are visible at the northeast end and a rippling effect inside the circuit walls implies underlying structures **(Fig. 7.7B).**

Excavation has traced a casemate wall — two parallel walls, with cross walls at intervals, creating rooms and giving a structure 5 m wide — enclosing an area of 140 x 80 m. It was entered through at least one monumental gate (at the northeast end). Both wall type and a six-roomed gate are similar to contemporary defensive walls at other sites of the Iron Age in Palestine and Transjordan. In the interior, excavation revealed a street and just outside the walled area has been found an important Nabataean building and rare examples of Thamudic and Latin inscriptions.

Finds from the site have been rich, including clay statuettes and a great deal of distinctive Moabite pottery (contrasting with the Ammonite forms which begin a little to the north).

This may be Jahaz, mentioned in the Hebrew Bible and on the Moabite Mesha stele. According to Numbers 21.21–4, Sihon of Heshbon met the Israelites in battle at Jahaz.

Fig. 7.7A: Khirbat el-Mudayna (APA98/ SL34.16, 20 May 1998)

Fig. 7.8B: El-Balu (APA98/ SL35.26, 20 May 1998)

Khirbat el-Balu

When Canon Tristram came this way in 1872 he observed: We 'passed through the ruins of Bal'hua, perhaps the poorest and most featureless we have seen'. As **Figure 7.8A** illustrates, the aerial view shows a rather different face to the world. It shows too, the significance of the location of this large prehistoric village: surrounded by the fertile Moabite plain and overlooking the Wadi Balu, which runs into the Wadi Mujib in the distance.

As so often in Jordan several periods are represented, from the Early Bronze Age (late 4th millennium BC) to the medieval Mamluk village in the southwest (12th–16th centuries AD). The major occupation, however, belongs to the Late Bronze and Iron Ages (16th–4th centuries BC), in particular the Moabite kingdoms of the Iron II period (*c.* 900–332 BC) when the settlement flourished.

The ruins stretch along the east side of the dark gash of the striking wadi. (The more limited traces on the north side seem to be mounds and enclosures, rather than buildings and include a large circle of orthostats). Settlement originated at the western end overlooking a shallow part of the wadi where it is joined by a tributary: there were once springs in that part of the wadi and there are still seasonal pools. This Iron Age village was surrounded by a casemate wall, traces of which can be seen as a double wall on the lower left and mid-right of **Figure 7.8B.** At its peak the Iron Age settlement of the 8th century BC extended for *c.* 450–500 m east–west. The largest Moabite settlement in the area and within the ring of border fortresses, Balu may have been a central place of the kingdom.

The great square mound of the Qasr is clear in the photograph — originally Iron Age in date and in the centre of the village which extended on either side. To the north and south of it are two large square towers; two others have also been reported. All around are clear traces of rectilinear buildings — some still standing to lintel height, with large open areas between. Especially notable is the much larger structure at the southwest edge (lower left), *c.* 20 m square. The rooms against the walls and central courtyard are characteristic of forts/caravanserais or major residences in several periods. Pottery in this area is largely Nabataean.

Balu is well known for the famous black basalt Balu Stela depicting a Moabite king and Egyptian deities. Recent excavation has revealed further powerful cultural links with Egypt as well as a later period of Assyrian and Babylonian domination.

Fig. 7.8A: El-Balu (APA98/ SL35.30, 20 May 1998)

Fig. 7.9B: Khirbat Mudeibi (APA98/ SL17.22, 14 May 1998)

Khirbat Mudeibi

Yet another Moabite fort: in this case, however, the fort is constructed on an open part of the plateau **(Fig. 7.9A).** As the view shows, it lies on a rise above a wadi.

Originally it seems to date from the Iron Age, but pottery from other periods, through to Islamic times, points to later use, too.

From the ground, the remains are visible and impressive, although the looping lines of animal 'corrals' made by modern Beduin confuse interpretation, and it is not possible to view the entire site from any direction. In the steeply oblique aerial view **(Fig. 7.9B)**, however, the lines of collapsed masonry immediately reveal an almost square fort, measuring 65 x 90 m. The thick outer wall is clear, and square towers can be seen at the corners, with others in between. There are gates in the middle of opposite sides. The monumental remains excavated at the east gate, imply that this was an important local centre.

The confusing wall lines inside the fort resolve themselves in this photograph into a large rectangular structure with a central courtyard, surrounded by rooms; its construction may be Nabataean.

The trenches of recent excavation can be seen inside the east gate (right) and across the north wall of the inner building. Outside the fort, the ancient dam across the wadi has been repaired to create the water supply that is vital in this arid region. The rectangular hole, just beyond the bottom left corner of the fort, may have been a cistern.

Fig. 7.9A: Khirbat Mudeibi (APA98/ SL17.20, 14 May 1998)

Fig. 7.10B: Khirbat Nahas: (APA98/ SL38.12, 20 May 1998)

Khirbat Nahas

The Arabic name — 'Copper Ruin' — explains why the site is in this deeply arid area. This is one of a series of centres of copper mining in the northeastern part of the Wadi Araba. A second centre, at the famous site of Faynan (Fig. 11.10) will be looked at later. In recent fieldwork, the workings at Khirbat Hamra Ifdan nearby have been proclaimed as the largest Bronze Age copper mine in the Middle East. Kh. Nahas is largely Iron Age though there are traces of earlier and later periods.

The character of the place is clear in **Figure 7.10A**: the rugged hills, bleak landscape and broad, but dry wadi, running down into the Rift Valley of the Wadi Araba. In the middle is the large copper working site, its features picked out by the dark mass of slag heaps and the redder outline of some of the buildings.

The site is large — about 10 ha: note the red pickup truck just right of the main enclosure. The main features stand out well. First, the great enclosure, described by an early commentator as being like 'a large prison camp'. It is *c.* 76 m square, the gate is probably on the northwest side (nearest the camera in **Fig. 7.10B**) and there are traces of structures (barracks for slaves?) inside. Southeast of the enclosure is a scatter of other well ordered, large, stone-built structures. Amongst them are small, square and circular smelting furnaces. Dominating the site are the black heaps of slag, defacing it even after almost three millennia. A modern calculation has concluded that 200,000 tons of slag, yielding *c.* 20,000 tons of copper, was extracted from the wider area of mining here. Kh. Nahas was one of the major components of this system.

Water must have been a serious problem. There is a small spring nearby, but totally inadequate. There are no traces yet of cisterns or reservoirs and the assumption is that work was seasonal when winter rains filled the wadi.

Fig. 7.10A: Khirbat Nahas: looking north (APA98/ SL38.9, 20 May 1998)

Fig. 8.1B: Petra: Khazneh (APA98/ SL39.20, 20 May 1998)

Petra

Petra is one of the best known archaeological sites in the world. Images of its monumental tombs are striking and familiar.

Part of the attraction of the site lies in its location. **Figure 8.1A** shows the broad valley set in its surrounding red sandstone mountain ring. It is arid, but water from a dam outside the mountains to the east (left) was led into the city through channels and tunnels. The entrance from Wadi Musa brings the visitor through the mountains on the left, down the narrow gorge of the Siq and then along a widening route; past the theatre cut into the living rock (left, just above the centre line; **Fig. 8.1F**) and on along the main paved street that runs across the photograph. On either side of this are public buildings under excavation — under the roof are the superb mosaics of the Late Roman church in which carbonized papyri were also found; to its right is the Temple of the Winged Lion; and opposite on the other side of the street is the so-called Great Temple. Finally the streets reached the tall walls of the Qasr el-Bint and, on the mountainside just beyond, the remains of a Crusader castle, el-Habis. Most of these ruins, including the so-called 'Roman Theatre', are in fact pre-Roman, the work of the talented Nabataeans in the 1st centuries BC and AD. The famous tombs are cut into the cliffs all around, the most extensive group being along the mountains on the left from the entrance, beyond the theatre in the shadow down to the bottom left corner.

The visitor coming down the Siq first encounters the Khazneh al-Faroun or 'Treasury of Pharaoh' **(Fig. 8.1B).** It was neither a treasury nor anything to do with an Egyptian pharaoh, but was built in the 1st century BC, probably for a Nabataean king. It is built in an embayment that restricts ground views. In the aerial view, the tomb seems small, almost hidden in a rocky cavern. The tiny human figures in front of it reveal the reality of an immense structure cut out of a still more immense rock formation, which continues to rise high above the architecture. More tombs can be seen beside where the track continues into the city.

In **Figure 8.1C** we are looking over a series of tombs, the theatre (late 1st century BC) and towards the temple known, misleadingly, as Qasr al-Bint Faroun ('The Palace (or Castle) of Pharaoh's Daughter') (1st century BC) in the distance (top right). Following this track, then looking back to the right, the visitor is confronted by a long line of major tombs **(Fig. 8.1E).** Most striking is the great platform in front of the Urn Tomb (1st century AD) — originally a royal tomb, in the 5th century AD it was converted into a church. Crowds of tourists reveal the immense size of these monuments.

Figure 8.1D looks north over the Great Temple (1st century BC and 1st century AD), and the paved and colonnaded street beyond, including the remains of an arched gate at its western (left) end. On the slope beyond is the Temple of the Winged Lion (early 1st century AD), which is dug out of the hillside. The same view shows the shops which once lined the street and traces of other structures on the slopes all around. Before excavation much of this central area of Petra looked featureless, but as archaeology has now revealed, it was crammed with public and domestic buildings of all kinds forming the city, which in turn, was surrounded by its 'city of the dead' cut into the mountainsides.

All around Petra are tombs cut into the rock, some now little more than caverns. On the hilltops are traces of altars and other 'high places' important to Nabataean religion, and free-standing obelisks, some cut from the living rock.

Best known of the more distant tombs is the Deir, 'The Monastery' **(Fig. 8.1F),** reached after a stiff climb up paths which often follow rock-cut staircases. It is a remarkable monument, superbly preserved and set in an isolated bay amongst the high mountains. The scale can be gauged from the human figures standing on top to the left. Once again it is Nabataean — in this case, 1st century AD.

Fig. 8.1C: Petra: panorama from the southeast (APA98/ SL39.24, 20 May 1998)

Fig. 8.1D: Petra: royal tombs with the Urn Tomb in the centre (APA98/ SL39.5, 20 May 1998)

Fig. 8.1E: Petra: Great Temple and Temple of the Winged Lion (APA98/ SL39.2, 20 May 1998)

Fig. 8.1F: Petra: Ed-Deir (APA98/ SL39.23, 20 May 1998)

Fig. 8.2B: Khirbat edh-Dharih (APA02.2/ SL27.33, 30 September, 2002)

Khirbat edh-Dharih

Lying in a fertile part of the Wadi La'aban, a tributary on the south side of the Wadi el-Hasa, this is one of the most attractive and exciting Nabataean sites in Jordan **(Fig. 8.2A).** Petra is about 100 km to the south and it is only an hour away from Kh. et-Tannur (Fig. 8.3) to the north overlooking the Wadi el-Hasa. The ancient King's Highway passed by it; springs provided a further attraction and survey has found numerous traces all around of ancient farmsteads, water collection systems, agriculture and quarries.

Figure 8.2A looks almost due north across the site, showing its commanding position on a spur overlooking the Wadi La'aban (left) as it runs down to the great Wadi el-Hasa (out of sight, above). Olive cultivation in the vicinity has re-emerged in modern times, hinting at the basis of the ancient economy. As the photograph shows, there is now a great deal to be seen. The site is about 500 m long by 200 m wide. Fortunately it has been extensively revealed through eleven seasons of excavation and consolidation. Other periods are represented — Pottery Neolithic, Bronze Age, Edomite and even a poor settlement of the Early Ottoman period (16th century AD). Overwhelmingly, however, this is a site which flourished in the Nabataean and Early Roman period.

The visible remains are of an important Nabataean temple and sanctuary on the tip of the spur, village houses all around, some with oil presses, a hostel for pilgrims, a caravanserai, and cemeteries to north and south. One of the latter is especially interesting — a deep rock-cut shaft containing several superimposed burials, some with associated coins.

The key structure is the great temple and sanctuary **(Fig. 8.2B),** transformed *c.* AD 100, from a simple shrine into a structure to rival those of Petra. It developed and flourished right through until the probable abandonment of the village at the time of the earthquake of 363. In short, it was a Nabataean temple, lavishly adorned with representations of deities and vegetal decoration, but reaching its peak in the Early Roman period. It was evidently of more than local significance. In the photograph can be seen both the northern entrance of the temple and the apse of the church later built inside it. The well-constructed rooms to the right are more functional and include one of the three oil presses found on the site.

Fig. 8.2A: Khirbat edh-Dharih (APA02.2/ SL28.1, 30 September, 2002)

Fig. 8.3B: Khirbat et-Tannur: looking west (APA98/ SL37.20, 20 May 1998)

Khirbat et-Tannur

This remarkable temple may have been the principal place of religious pilgrimage in the Nabataean kingdom outside Petra. Certainly its location makes it one of the most visually stunning archaeological sites in Jordan **(Fig. 8.3A)**. The tall conical hill on which it was built, lies *inside* the rim of the Wadi el-Hasa, which it overlooks from the south. The hill dominates the valley from its summit — *c.* 700 m above sea level and 400 metres above the Wadi el-Hasa itself. Access is difficult even today; a narrow track from the southeast is visible in the photograph, coming in at the bottom right.

The site consists only of the temple complex, 40 x 48 m overall. Unlike Khirbat edh-Dharih, 7 km to the south, there is no associated settlement. This was a sacred place, a shrine which attracted pilgrims who made offerings and who could be accommodated. The structure is often referred to as being like a Russian doll — in this case, the three successive phases being most prominent with the altar itself. In the second photograph **(Fig. 8.3B)**, the small square of the altar can be seen in the centre of the large square. The altar began as a simple structure at which devotees would make burnt offerings (some of which — animals bones and cereals — were found deposited under the courtyard). In the next phase a larger structure was built all around the altar and the bulk of the rest of the complex was added. Finally, the altar was again sheathed in a further structure and raised in height, so that its upper surface was 3–4 m high and had to be reached by a staircase. The altar itself and the surrounding room were ornately decorated with elaborate floral and human relief sculpture. The latter included the deities being worshipped — Qos-Dushara and his consort; here represented in the form of the Syrian deities Hadad and Atargatis.

This altar room was fronted with a large square courtyard, which had a covered colonnade along either side. Beyond this flanking colonnade, as can be seen, were two ranges of rectilinear rooms on either side. On the left one is a long hall, while those on the right are smaller, squarer and include one tacked onto the front wall (bottom right) outside the main enclosure. They will have served as accommodation for pilgrims and the rooms in which they could pursue the ritual feasting associated with worship.

Dating has varied. The most recent argues that Phase I was of the late 1st century BC, with Phase II and the main developments coming a century later, towards the end of the 1st century AD.

Fig. 8.3A: Khirbat et-Tannur: looking north towards the Wadi-el-Hasa (APA98/ SL37.21, 20 May 1998)

Fig. 8.7B: Khirbat el-Moreighah: near vertical view looking east (APA98/ SL40.11, 20 May 1998)

Kh. el-Moreighah

The high oblique view **(Fig. 8.7A)** includes both a site and one of the most enigmatic ancient features in Jordan.

The Khatt Shebib is the name given to the wall which comes in at the bottom left, is interrupted beside the ruins, continues beyond them for some length before changing direction and running off into the distance. It is a long wall of basalt boulders, which meanders southwards along, broadly, the boundary between steppe and desert in this area of Jordan, east and southeast of Petra. A stretch has long been known beginning *c.* 15 km due west of Ma'an and ending just northwest of Kh. Dauq, on the edge of the Shera'a escarpment. That is about 30 km but in fact there are further gaps, then long extensions, giving a feature as much as 160 km in length. The wall is undated but often presented as medieval. In fact, an earlier date, perhaps Nabataean, is likely.

The ruins astride the wall are those of Khirbat el-Moreighah. As the low-level oblique photograph shows **(Fig. 8.7B),** it is a large site of about 1 hectare, the core of which is some 120 m (NS) by about 90 m (EW), with a few outlying structures. The aerial view is instructive, showing graphically the location of the site on the top of the low hill and the nature of the undulating country all around. Even in the oblique view the site appears a little different from the old sketch plan of 1935. The latter is a useful generalized drawing of a site whose walls must have been difficult to interpret at ground level. It is evident from the photograph **(Fig. 8.7B)** that the site looks very much as if it is distorted by later building — a large rectangular structure, subsequently partly overbuilt with individual smaller buildings straddling its circuit.

The rectangular enclosure is substantial — about 100 x 60 m, 0.6 ha/1.5 acres. It looks very like a defensive circuit for a small fort, or buildings arranged facing inwards, to create a rectangular arrangement. The major later structures are those along part of the south wall **(Fig. 8.7B)** (right), that at the northwest corner (bottom left) and the very large building straddling the east wall (far side). The last of these is some 40 x 50 m and consists of several large rooms.

From the outset Moreighah has been interpreted as a Nabataean site; there is a little Iron Age pottery, but otherwise it is exclusively Nabataean material. The evidence for overbuilding points to later use of the site. Importantly, too, for dating the Khatt Shebib, the disappearance of that wall on either side of Moreighah is surely because its stones were removed to construct one of the phases of the fort/ settlement. In short, the Khatt Shebib must be Nabataean or earlier.

Fig. 8.7A: Khirbat el-Moreighah: looking south (APA98/ SL40.9, 20 May 1998)

Fig. 8.8A: Umm el-Tawabin: looking southwest (APA98/ SL37.31, 20 May 1998)

Umm el-Tawabin

This is a remarkable site for its location and features. **Figure 8.8A** shows the setting, on the east side of the Wadi Araba, just south of Es-Safi and the Dead Sea. To the west (top right) lie fields belonging to the settlements of the fertile lands of the Southern Ghors. To the east (bottom left), the craggy hills rise up steeply to the Shera'a Plateau, several hundred metres higher. The ancient site is close by where the major Wadi el-Hasa joins the Wadi Araba and lies at minus 200 m below sea level.

The ruins are unusual and varied. In a landscape where so much is regular, we are confronted with a defensive wall which snakes its way around the lower slopes of an elongated outcrop. The wall can be seen starting just left of centre, as a dark brown strip, just above the very pale outcrops on the hillside. It runs south, before looping back round the far side of the hill, down towards the right corner. It does not enclose the hill entirely, but still runs for no less than *c.* 2.5 km. Although it is described as a 'fortress', the incomplete circuit and the location on a natural edge suggest it is more an enclosure than a serious defence. In general appearance, the wall is most immediately reminiscent of the walls built by the Romans around their camps and for circumvallation around the Jewish fortress of Masada.

In the second photograph **(Fig. 8.8B),** we are looking down the length of the site. In the foreground is the start of a string of two or three dozen small circular enclosures on both sides of the circuit wall. Most are *c.* 2–3 m in diameter, but a few are larger. They have openings on the northeast side in each case. The principal explorer of the site suggested they revealed where tents had once stood. He also recorded other structures inside, especially to the south and west, including a reservoir. One structure can be seen on the crest at the far end (south) and another close to the wall on the right (west). No less interesting is the circuit wall just beside the latter — there appear to be two towers flanking a possible entrance.

Pottery of the Chalcolithic to Mamluk periods is present, but the explorer believes it is 'predominantly' a large Nabataean site.

Fig. 8.8B: Umm el-Tawabin: looking south (APA98/ SL37.29, 20 May 1998)

Fig. 8.9B: Qasr et-Telah: looking north over the fort and reservoir (APA98/ SL38.1, 20 May 1998)

Qasr et-Telah

Just east of the highway running the length of the Wadi Araba and 25 km south of the Dead Sea, is the remarkable fort and settlement of Qasr et-Telah. It comprises a small fort, a reservoir and aqueduct, and an extensive area of regular fields which are apparently very old **(Fig. 8.9A).**

It is the last of these which has long caught attention and the other features remain strangely unstudied. **Figure 8.9A** shows the fields as they are now being re-used. The modern boundaries respect the ancient and one can still see the irregular, but orderly division of a large area into long strips and in many cases can also see the vertical divisions, which created rectangular fields. This fossilized field system is defined by nearly straight banks 50–100 cm wide, creating a checkerboard pattern covering an area of *c.* 1000 x 600 m, *c.* 60 ha in total. A 'typical' field at Qasr et-Telah is about 32 x 52 m (*c.* 0.1664 ha).

In the second photograph **(Fig. 8.9B),** we are looking almost vertically down into the fort and reservoir. The fort (left) is an enclosure, *c.* 40 m sq, walls 2 m thick, and corner towers 4 m square and projecting 2.8 m. The air photograph shows traces of internal buildings, built against at least the east and north walls. The reservoir nearby is almost exactly 34 m square and is fed by the aqueduct, several hundred metres long, coming in from the Wadi et-Telah at the southeast corner (bottom right).

The site is commonly identified with a Roman garrison place named in a document of *c.* AD 400: in it we are told there is 'The Ala Constantiana [a cavalry regiment], at Toloha'; it may be the 'Dhat Atlah' mentioned in connection with a Muslim expedition of AD 629. Certainly surface pottery of the Roman and Umayyad periods is present, but the earliest exploration there found only Nabataean pottery and a coin. As at the next site and elsewhere in Jordan (e.g. Fig. 10.3), this may be best interpreted as a significant Nabataean site which remained in occupation during succeeding centuries and was at one point a Roman military post, too.

Fig. 8.9A: Qasr et-Telah: looking northwest over the ancient field system (APA98/ SL38.3, 20 May 1998)

Fig. 8.10B: 'Jardines romaines': looking northeast (APA00/ SL6.19 (RHB), 14 September 2000)

Khirbat Debdebah and 'Jardins romaines'

The Nabataeans are rightly famous for their skill in harvesting and storing water and for exploiting it for agricultural purposes. In practice, they were building on many centuries of gradual development in hydraulic skills going back to the Bronze Age. Nevertheless, the extent of Nabataean settlement and the impressive works associated with their sites in arid regions underscores their achievement. Best known are the farms along the wadis of the Negev Desert, but further traces can be found widely in Jordan, not least in the vicinity of Petra itself. As with field systems anywhere, their dating is very problematic. And as so often in Jordan with this period, pottery of the Nabataean period is often found with that of the subsequent periods, implying continued use and obscuring the origins.

In one of the broad valleys northeast of Petra lies the deserted village of Debdebah. Travellers in the early 19th century reported it as still occupied intermittently by local Christians, but examination in the 1930s revealed Nabataean pottery. The site lies amongst the trees above and to the right of the centre of **Figure 8.10A.** As the photograph shows, it is accompanied by an impressive swathe of terraced fields, of irregular shapes and sizes, sweeping down towards the viewer. Although under cultivation again today, they are ancient and certainly associated with the farm/ hamlet of Debdebah.

There are fields north and northwest of Petra too, but of particular interest are those characterized by French archaeologists as 'Jardins romaines' west of Petra. The air photograph **(Fig. 8.10B)** shows extensive traces of decayed fields along the western end of the Wadi Musa, for about 1,200 metres. Again there are small irregular fields on the higher terraces, but also others formed by walls across, at least parts, of the wadi. Also visible are long walls for channelling water from the wadi onto the fields.

Fig. 8.10A: Debdebah: looking east (APA98/ SL39.28, 20 May 1998)

9. GREEKS AND ROMANS

'[Arabia] also has, in addition to some towns, great cities, Bostra, Gerasa and Philadelphia, all strongly defended by mighty walls' (Ammianus Marcellinus 14.8.13; 4th century AD; Loeb trans)

Greeks had been present as traders in the Near East as early as the Mycenaean Bronze Age. In the 8th century BC and later, Greeks re-appeared as traders and as mercenaries and by the 5th century regularly took service with the armies of the kings of Achaemenid Persia. The superiority of the Greek 'way of war' was illustrated still further with the campaigns of Alexander the Great, which brought all of Western Asia under Macedonian Greek rule. Now Greeks came to settle and did so in large numbers. New cities sprang up. Scores were founded by Alexander and his immediate successors, others followed in later generations. The settlers were often military colonists, but there is good evidence that the new cities could include significant numbers of non-Greeks, drawn from the indigenous population. These new populations, Hellenistic rather than Hellenic, developed their distinctive cultures and, despite remaining a modest minority in the Near East as a whole, they dominated politically and culturally.

Hellenism was relatively late in arriving in Jordan. There were early military expeditions against the Nabataeans, but the first 'Greek' cities are generally dated to the later 3rd or 2nd centuries BC. Most bear the distinctive dynastic or Macedonian names one finds elsewhere: Antioch (Gerasa, modern Jarash), Philadelphia (Amman), Pella (Tabaqat Fahl), and Gadara (Umm Qeis) are amongst the Decapolis cities in Jordan. An indirect strand of Hellenism entered Jordan through two other avenues: first, the Jewish settlements of the Hasmonaean and Herodian dynasties; second, the impact of the great Hellenistic city of Alexandria in Egypt on the Nabataeans and, in particular, their architecture at Petra.

This was an increasingly cosmopolitan world of natives, Jews, Macedonians and Greeks, of influences surviving from the region itself and those imported from Mesopotamia; all now being transformed under the impact of the Hellenism flowing in from the west.

Romans, too, settled in the Near East. Some had been present as businessmen before the creation of the first province (Syria) in 63 BC; most came later as soldiers and many stayed as discharged veterans. Roman soldiers could be Italians, especially if serving in the legions. Most, however, were of provincial extraction. Consequently, most veterans settling in the region — all of them by definition Roman citizens — were from almost every part of the empire: Gauls, Egyptians, Thracians, Africans ... as well as Italians.

The Romans also created new cities, but the principle Roman contribution was in what happened to the existing ones. Urban development, rather than urbanization. It was under Roman rule that the cities grew, developed and flourished; bigger, grander, more monumental and often enormously impressive. Before the present, Jordan was never to be more urbanized than during the centuries of Roman rule. The first phase of development was during the 1st and 2nd centuries AD, but a second phase came after the christianising of the empire, when the new religion brought about the transformation of the architectural landscape, with its distinctive building types — the churches that blossomed in the 5th, 6th and early 7th centuries in particular.

Beyond the cities lay even more numerous towns, villages and farmsteads, as well as the entire infrastructure of roads, road-stations and bridges, that made the Roman period so developed, so 'modern' in appearance.

Fig. 9.1B: Site 1 at the Kafrein Dam: looking west (APA98/ SL27.29, 17 May 1998)

'Iraq al-Amir (ancient Tyros) and a Fort in the Wadi Kafrein

The lush valley of Wadi es-Sir lies 18 km west of Amman, on an ancient road linking it to Jerusalem. The remains at 'Iraq al-Amir include a village, farms and fortifications scattered over a wide area. There are traces of settlement from early prehistory to the present day, including the Babylonian and Achaemenid Persian periods that are often poorly attested. The best known element is the gleaming white building on a slight rise southwest of the village, known as Qasr al-'Abd ('The Fort of the Servant') **(Fig. 9.1A)**. Ironically, what is one of the most striking Hellenistic structures in Jordan, is the work of a non-Greek.

The place is in fact well-known from ancient literary sources, which describe how members of the aristocratic Jewish Tobiad family — originally Persian appointees — were engaged as tax collectors in Transjordan on behalf of the Hellenistic Ptolemies, who ruled Egypt and parts of Palestine and southern Syria. The advance of the Seleucid rulers of Syria led eventually, in the 170s BC, to the last of this Tobiad family, Hyrcanus, moving permanently to his manor house at the place they called Tyros. It is described by the late 1st century AD Jewish historian Josephus: 'And he built a strong fortress, which was constructed entirely of white marble up to the very roof, and had beasts of gigantic size carved on it, and he enclosed it with a wide and deep moat' (*Antiquities* XII.230, Loeb trans.). This was a world of revived urbanism and cities of a new kind at one of which — Philadelphia (Amman) — these Tobiads played a role. Josephus described this Tyros as a fortified residence, with villas and parks in the vicinity, and we now know there was also a village.

The fortified residence was never completed, but it was far advanced when work was abandoned. Extensive reconstruction has produced an impressive, though roofless, building. The general form of the building (37 x 18.5 m) has parallels from the region, as well as parallels for such fortified manors in contemporary northern Iraq and Iran. The architectural decoration however, is powerfully influenced from the great Hellenistic centre of Alexandria. There are Corinthian columns on the façade and parts of the upper story, and lions and eagles in relief decorate the exterior. From the air this rare example of an aristocratic manor house is the striking feature of the valley, and it dominates the landscape of agricultural lands. In antiquity, when springs in the surrounding hills fed water into the surrounding lake, it would have left an impression of a building almost floating on water, like one of the great pleasure boats of the contemporary Ptolemies in Egypt.

The Wadi es-Sir joins the Wadi Kafrein, and 12 km southwest of 'Iraq al-Amir, a group of defended sites are clustered alongside this wadi near the modern Kafrein Dam. One of those explored recently has been identified as a Hellenistic period fort. The near-vertical view **(Fig. 9.1B)** shows the rectangular enclosure (*c.* 40 x 30 m) on the summit of a hill with the recent ditches of the landscapers. The corners have massive square projecting towers and there is a huge circular well in the courtyard. Internally there seem to have been few significant structures, but the excavators found extensive traces of burning and numerous whole or shattered pottery vessels implying sudden destruction. The site was an important strategic point in several periods — there is an Iron Age fort; two Hasmonaean-Roman period 'forts' are located nearby, the Ottomans occupied the area in the 19th century and the Jordan army was there until recently.

Fig. 9.1A: Qasr al-Abd, 'Iraq al-Amir: looking northwest over the Hellenistic fortified mansion of the Tobiad family (APA98/ SL27.18, 17 May 1998)

Fig. 9.2B: Ain ez-Zara: looking southeast (APA98/ SL29.26, 17 May 1998)

Ain es-Zara

The eastern shore of the Dead Sea is marked by a series of wadis plunging down *c.* 1,000 m from the plateau above. Together with springs along the shore, a number of places were singled out for settlement through the proliferation of water sources. The healing properties of the hot springs (42° to 64° C) at one of these **(Fig. 9.2A),** 2 km south of the gorge of the Wadi Zarqa Ma'in, attracted Herod the Great, who was taken there in the months before his death in 4 BC. In fact there are some 40 springs of varying temperatures and properties. These may be the Kallirrhoe (literally the 'Beautiful Springs') mentioned in ancient texts, and depicted on the mosaic map of Madaba — as a vignette of three buildings and palm trees, situated between two gorges, presumably the Zarqa Ma'in and the Wadi Mujib.

Until recently this area was inaccessible by modern transport and the best approach was from the western shore of the Dead Sea. However, the construction of the modern road, bringing with it a certain amount of destruction, has allowed archaeologists to survey and excavate the ruins surrounding the thermal springs, uncovering the remains of Roman occupation.

The central area of the excavations — marked out by the box grid of excavation — has revealed a rectangular structure (right) **(Fig. 9.2B)** dating to the Early Roman period. In parts there were the remains of a white plastered floor, with pottery and glass fragments dating from the Roman period and the earliest coins from the site date to the years 5 and 4 BC. The style and elaborate decoration are best paralleled in Herodian buildings in Israel and it is probably a *villa maritima* of Herodian date.

At the edge of the shore there is also evidence of a harbour, and recent investigations have identified early Roman villas/ farms (left). Once again the rich soils, together with the abundant water, made this an attractive area for settlement and explain the interest, not just of Herod, but later wealthy landowners.

The ancient settlement and springs was surrounded by a massive stone wall, encircling the fields as well as the houses and baths; it may have a perimeter of 2,200 m.

Fig. 9.2A: Ain ez-Zara: looking north (APA98/ SL29.30, 17 May 1998)

Fig. 9.3B: Amman: forum, theatre and odeon complex, looking northwest (APA98/SL43.14, 21 May 1998)

Amman

Visitors to Jordan will first encounter the Graeco-Roman world in the national capital itself. The modern name echoes that of its distant Bronze and Iron Age predecessor, Rabbat Ammon. It emerged as a Graeco-Roman city after refoundation in the time of the Hellenistic Egyptian king, Ptolemy II Philadelphus (282–246 BC), who called it Philadelphia, a name it was to retain for a thousand years. The re-emergence of the more ancient name in the immediate post-Roman period — as happened also at Jarash and elsewhere — suggests that whatever the official name on the lips of the ruling power and the Graeco-Roman citizens the mass of native inhabitants never ceased to think of it as Ammon.

The modern city now dwarfs and largely obscures the ancient city **(Fig. 9.3A).** Although little is known of the houses or work places of the population, major elements of its great public buildings have survived and from time to time rich churches or suburban villas are uncovered in the wider area, hinting at the scatter of villages and farms that once surrounded it. The prosperity that can be read, even in the surviving fragments, was based on the fertile farming lands all around, as well as on its location at a fork where the King's Highway and the Roman *Via Nova Traiana* diverged. It was probably an assize centre in the Roman period and we have inscriptions, some in Latin, referring to soldiers of the Roman army based there, as well as a few recruited there.

Hellenistic Amman is almost invisible. There are plenty of artefacts from excavations and we have papyri from Egypt of the early 3rd century BC listing people with Greek names, some described as *klerucbs,* military colonists, and referring to Birta Ammanitis, 'The Fortress (and Administrative centre) of Ammon'. In the air photo **(Fig. 9.3A)** the core of the Hellenistic and Roman city stands out. This is the citadel, the present el-Qal'a. It dominates the areas in the valleys below, where the town grew up and developed. The walls are Hellenistic in date and the great temple of Hercules, whose columns can be seen at the far end of the plateau, has been dated to AD 161–169. Also visible is the later church of St Elianos, to the left of the temple just in front of the buses. Most of the rest is Umayyad, dominated by the magnificent palace, whose domed hall has been restored.

The same photograph, shows part of the great theatre in the valley in the distance (top left). A steep oblique view **(Fig. 9.3B)** reveals the scale and magnificence of this entire complex. Dominating the group is the theatre, 74 m in diameter, seating about 6,000. To its right, is a small odeon of a type common in these Decapolis cities (Figs 9.4–9.6; 11.2A); it is 36 m in diameter and could seat about 1,200. Both are dated to the second half of the 2nd century AD. Less evident, but crucial to the complex, is the forum, the rectangular area between the two theatres, and once again today a public meeting place. Some of the columns lining one side of the forum can be seen just in front of the theatre. The modern road, at the top of the photograph, roughly follows one of the main streets of the ancient city. A second, going off down to the left, ran past the still visible remains of an immense nymphaeum, an ornamental fountain.

Fig. 9.3A: Amman: citadel, looking southeast (APA98/SL43.7, 21 May 1998)

Fig. 9.4B: Jarash: northern cardo, temple of Artemis and north theatre, looking south (APA98/SL24.22, 16 May 1998)

Jarash

After Petra, Jarash is the best-known archaeological site in Jordan. Less than an hour's drive from Amman, the visitor moves from a city on the very edge of the steppe to one nestling in a highland basin. To reach it one crosses the perennial River Zarqa (the Biblical Jabbok) and follows the increasingly leafy road beside its tributary, the Wadi Jarash. Jarash itself lies where the valley broadens in the heart of a great basin in the hills; secluded, cool, well-watered from rain, the river and numerous springs, and with rich *terra rosa* soils. It is no surprise the early settlers were delighted by the spot and called the modest stream the 'Golden River'.

Archaeologists have found extensive traces of settlement in the area from at least the Bronze Age and there was Iron Age settlement too. By the 3rd century BC, the place was probably a town, or at least a strongpoint in the midst of farming villages. In the early 2nd century BC it was refounded as a Hellenistic city; 'Antioch on the Chrysorroas, also called Gerasa' is how it appears on a later inscription. Gerasa is certainly a Semitic name and its persistence implies that the pre-Greek settlement was a significant one and that the later inhabitants were happy to still call it by its old name. Presumably because they themselves were Semitic, or of very mixed background.

Gerasa flourished for several centuries under Roman rule and in the 1st to 3rd centuries acquired most of its main structures. The roll call is impressive: the Oval Piazza (1st century AD), a gridded street plan (late 2nd century), South Theatre (late 1st century), a city wall 3.456 km long encircling an area of just over 80 ha/ 200 acres (early 2nd century), two monumental gates (North: AD 115; South: Hadrianic), a triumphal arch (AD 129/30), hippodrome (mid-2nd century) the immense Temple of Zeus (1st century, but monumentalized in the 160s), of Artemis (monumentalized AD 150–80), North Theatre (160s), West and East Baths (late 2nd century?), as well as the programmes to transform the main streets into splendid colonnaded ways with monuments at their junctions (late 1st and 2nd centuries). In the Late Roman period came a spate of churches — ultimately 15 we know of, many with glittering multi-coloured mosaics. The city continued to prosper in the early Umayyad period, but then went into decline. A Crusader historian, William of Tyre, could describe it as deserted in AD 1122. Western travellers rediscovered it and wrote glowingly about it in the 19th century. Soon after, a colony of Circassians was established in the eastern half of the ruins. The modern town has spread over most of this area, but the western half remains free from development.

Figure 9.4A shows Roman Jarash as most modern visitors now encounter it coming from Amman. Emerging from the beautiful leafy upper valley of the Wadi Jarash, one arrives face to face with the Arch of Hadrian and the rear wall of the little hippodrome, both now extensively restored. The road along the right side of the latter, links the triumphal arch to the South Gate, which is almost a replica. Inside the gate lie three of the most famous monuments. To the left is the immense Temple of Zeus and beyond it (not shown) the South Theatre, with seating for 6,000. Directly in front is the unique Oval Piazza **(Cover**

continued on page 170...

Fig. 9.4A: Jarash: the arch of Hadrian, the hippodrome and the city beyond, looking northwest (APA98/SL25.2, 17 May 1998)

Fig. 9.5B: Pella: The mound of Tabaqat Fahl, looking west (APA98/ SL22.33, 16 May 1998)

Pella (modern Tabaqat Fahl)

The city is located 33 km northwest of Jarash where the ancient route along the Wadi Jirm el-Moz emerges from the hills, before crossing the plain to the River Jordan 4 km further on **(Fig. 9.5A).** Extensive excavation has revealed settlement, in an area of strong springs, as early as the Palaeolithic. There was an early city there in the Middle and Late Bronze Age which had contacts with contemporary Egypt and appears in the latter's records. The place may have been abandoned in the Late Iron Age; certainly the Hellenistic settlement that re-appeared in the 3rd century BC seems to have been a new urban venture. Although the new name evoked the city of that name in Macedonia, it may have been a play on the older native name which has survived to this day as Tabaqat Fahl. The Graeco-Roman and Umayyad city had a continuous history of a thousand years, but was devastated by an earthquake in AD 746/7. There was still significant settlement in the Abassid and Mamluk periods and settlement of sorts right through to modern times, though the great city was long gone. The site today is not overbuilt and ruins can be seen on the main mound, on the adjacent Tell el-Husn and to some extent on neighbouring hills and their intervening valleys.

The core of the Roman ruins is visible in **Figure 9.5A**. In the left foreground is Tell el-Husn with exposed foundations on the summit and slopes. Just visible on the right is the edge of Tabaqat Fahl itself, the largely artificial mound created by centuries of settlement. The visible remains of the Roman city lie in the lush valley between the two hills creating what is known as the Civic Complex. Clearest is the poorly preserved small theatre, the Odeon, dated to the late 1st/ early 2nd century AD and capable of seating *c.* 1,000. Here too lay an early Roman bath building; columns to the right of the Odeon are those of a Late Roman church, perhaps the city's cathedral. In practice, the early Roman remains are still relatively poorly revealed — we would expect a second and larger theatre, and one only has to compare Jarash to see how much more there could be.

In **Figure 9.5B** we are looking down over Tabaqat Fahl. The white modern building on its plateau is the 'dig house' of the American and Australian excavators. Again trenches have left foundations exposed, but if the eye follows along the left edge of the mound beyond these, traces of structures not yet explored can be seen eroding out of the surface.

Fig. 9.5A: Pella: the civic complex nestled between Tell el-Husn and the mound of Tabaqat Fahl, looking west (APA98/ SL22.31, 16 May 1998)

Fig. 9.6B: Gadara: the acropolis with Ottoman Village, theatres and a civic complex, looking southeast (APA98/SL43.32, 21 May 1998)

Gadara (modern Umm Qeis)

This famous Decapolis city lies in a commanding and spectacular position. To the north is the deep valley of the Wadi Yarmuk, to the west is the Jordan valley and the outlook to the northwest is over the Golan Heights and Sea of Galilee. The Hellenistic city was founded in the 3rd century BC, but the Semitic root of the name 'Gadara' means 'fortification' and probably implies an earlier military post. Although it had a dynastic name — both Antioch and Seleucia are attested — the older Semitic name, Gadara, was the one in common use, perhaps suggesting an even less hellenized population than in other Decapolis cities. On the other hand, it produced several notable figures in the arts and sciences. Occupation continued strongly in the Umayyad period. The modest settlement of later periods gave way in Ottoman times to the large village of Umm Qeis — itself now a heritage site — overlying the eastern end of the town, where the core of the town clustered around a hill, the ancient acropolis.

The city itself is elongated, stretching along a flat-topped ridge with ruins extended over 1.6 km. The walled area of the town is a smaller, irregular area of about 700 x 300 m. Like Jarash it has a rich architectural heritage from its Roman period: two theatres, baths, temples, a nymphaeum, colonnaded streets and shops, tombs, a hippodrome (never completed), city gates and a monumental arch/ gateway straddling the road west. As at Jarash, there is a third, smaller theatre, to the north of the city (in this case at the hot springs and bath of Hammeth sadar, in Israel).

Figure 9.6A shows the approach from the west and the Jordan Valley, with the outline of the incomplete hippodrome and a monumental gate just beyond. Following the road towards the camera brings the traveller into the city.

Figure 9.6B looks down over the acropolis (*c.* 250 x 250 m) showing how much higher the ground is here. There is a section of excavated Hellenistic city wall of the 2nd century BC on its south side. One can see too, why the Ottoman village retreated to this spot in modern times. The houses of the latter are largely built out of ancient masonry, the distinctive black basalt of the area. The acropolis hill is the location of some of the most notable Greek and early Roman structures. Just visible at the top left, as a grass-covered bowl on the right side of the rectangular car park, is the large North Theatre (1st century BC/ early 1st century AD), which looks north over what we now know was a large Hellenistic temple precinct, the podium of whose temple is 2nd century BC. On the right is the small West Theatre (2nd century AD), well preserved and being restored. Running down from the East Gate and in front of the North Theatre is the start of the colonnaded Decumanus, which can be traced on across the city and out past the hippodrome as far as the arch/ gateway, 1.7 km to the west, where there may have been an ancient customs post **(Fig. 9.6A).** At the point where the Decumanus meets the road from the West Theatre, there is a nymphaeum (late 2nd century AD) part of whose apsidal foundation can be seen at the roadside opposite the junction.

In the centre foreground, just left of the West Theatre, is a remarkable complex of civic buildings: an octagonal Basilica (early 6th century AD) with a further church (late 6th century AD) behind and a colonnaded courtyard in front. The terraced platform on which they stand, however, is early Roman in date. Along the street front are the openings of 20 vaulted shops, reconstructed from the remains found lying on the street where the frontages had collapsed in an 8th century AD earthquake. These too, are late in date, but they are the rebuild of earlier examples.

Fig. 9.6A: Gadara: the unfinished hippodrome foundations and the monumental gate, looking southeast (APA98/SL22.10, 16 May 1998)

Fig. 9.7B: At-Tuwana: the 'fort' (APA02.2/ SL26.16, 30 September 2002)

At-Tuwana (Thana/ Thoana/ Thornia)

This is one of the more enigmatic sites in Jordan **(Fig. 9.7A).** Lying east of the major modern town of Tafila, in south central Jordan, one is immediately struck by two features. First, the landscape seems arid and uninviting. Yet the plateau in this area has, in fact, a high rainfall (*c.* 400 mm) and the immediate vicinity is renowned for its fruit trees. Second, the extent and quality of preservation would seem to invite exploration. Yet little has been written about it.

Published descriptions from ground visits are enthusiastic, but give little scope for visualizing the site as a whole or understanding its components. The aerial view is a classic example of how a site can be much easier to understand from a single high view.

At-Tuwana is a small town, *c.* 800 x 450 m, *c.* 36 ha almost half the size of Jarash (Fig. 9.4) and a little smaller than Umm el-Jimal (Fig. 11.3). The alignment was evidently determined by the ancient route which ran north–south through the valley. In the Roman period the route became a part of the *Via Nova Traiana* (Fig. 9.10A). In the late 1980s the modern track through the site was, unfortunately, replaced with a new surfaced road, which sliced through ancient structures on a new alignment.

The major features are clear. Structures are scattered over a wide area, on high ground, on either side of the road. Although they are almost all rectilinear, those on the southeast are generally larger units and set out in an orderly fashion, broadly aligned on the road. In contrast, note the smaller sizes and appearance of organic growth to the northwest and in the foreground on the southeast. The latter look like clusters of rooms and are reminiscent of the houses at Umm el-Jimal. Around the exterior of the structures as a whole are a series of enclosures which are probably fields. Numerous cisterns have been reported and appear on the photograph as black dots where the deep shade of the opening is captured; there are several dry reservoirs.

The dominant structure is the large rectangular enclosure which may be the one described by ground visitors as *c.* 120 x 80 m **(Fig. 9.7B).** It has been suggested as a caravanserai. An alternative is to view it as a Roman fort, later given over to other uses and around which a town grew up. The interior has various walled open spaces, but also significant traces of buildings. One has substantial standing walls, highlighted by the sun, and appears to be divided into three aisles. Although no apse is visible, one might think of a church there. Beside it are traces of other buildings and it may be part of a complex. The large square ruin to its left may be the 'temple' one traveller suggested. Pottery from the site includes some Iron Age and quantities of Umayyad and Mamluk. Most, however, is Nabataean and Roman, with an apparent tail off towards the end of the Roman period.

Fig. 9.7A: At-Tuwana, looking north (APA02.2/ SL26.30, 30 September 2002)

Fig. 9.8A: Er-Rabbah: temple and colonnaded street (APA02.2/SL22.19, 30 September 2002)

Er-Rabbah (ancient Rabbathmoab; Areopolis)

This is one of those marvellous sites with which Jordan can constantly surprise. Simple modern villages turn out to have an ancient core, with traces of old structures incorporated in modern houses; a column drum here or piece of architrave or inscription there. With Rabbah one has a bonus.

The place is well-known. It was Rabbathmoab of the Nabataeans and, along with Petra (Fig. 8.1), Characmoab (Fig. 13.1) and Bostra, was one of the four principal centres of the new province, created in AD 106, when Rome annexed the Nabataean kingdom. A recently published papyrus dated AD 127 reports a Roman cavalry regiment in garrison and the place being used as a centre for a census taking; it was probably also an assize centre. That would make sense, because it also lay directly on the ancient King's Highway, reconstructed and renamed the *Via Nova Traiana* by the Romans (Fig. 9.10A). In the same century it struck its own coins for a time and took the romanized name, Areopolis, 'City of Ares/Mars'. In about AD 400 a regiment was again stationed there. In short, this was an important early Roman town and garrison place.

In the 19th century travellers often remarked on the significant remains there. This is Canon Tristram who was there in 1872:

The place seems to have been square, with the Roman road almost intersecting it from north to south; and the course of the main street may be traced. ... The Roman town seems to have been about three-quarters of a mile each way. There are several huge grassgrown mounds, evidently the tombs of some important buildings, which might well repay excavation. One temple has two Corinthian columns standing, and portions of several others, with two arches. There are also two other large open tanks, but all else is only a mass of walls, broken-down fragments of carved work, and Corinthian capitals; broken sarcophagi here and there, blocks of basalt, vaults and arched cellars of all sizes, ... These vaults are countless. The Romans have evidently used in their construction many carved stones from yet earlier edifices. The material of the city is limestone. But we found many blocks of basalt, which must have been brought from Shihan, several miles off, built into the walls and arches, some of them finely faced, and others carved, telling of a still more ancient Moabite city. Among the blocks of basalt thus used were fragments of architraves and entablatures. Several of the sarcophagi were of basalt also, but without sculpture. At the eastern end of the city are the remains of a large square building, which seems, by some bases left in situ, *to have had a colonnade round a central court, probably the praetorium.*

The modern traveller arriving in this little Jordanian town will see far less than was visible to Tristram, but will still be rewarded with the striking remains.

In **Figure 9.8A** the roofless Roman temple catches the eye. All around are traces of other ruins including just to the left, beside the modern highway, the stretch of paved road where the Roman *Via Nova Traiana* becomes the main street of the town. Even this provincial town had a colonnaded street — re-erected columns are visible. In the panoramic view **(Fig. 9.8B)** are three successive reservoirs — Tristram's 'cisterns': a medium square one, a small square one beyond that and a large square one further away still. The picture tells a further story — rich farmland explains the location and the prosperity of the place.

Fig. 9.8B: Er-Rabbah: looking southwest of the modern town with the Roman temple, colonnaded streets and reservoirs (APA98/SL36.5, 20 May 1998)

Tombs

Beyond the walls of every Classical city lie the necropoleis, the 'Cities of the Dead'. Jarash was no different and over the course of its thousand year history, with a population at its height of up to 10,000, between 100,000 and 200,000 people died. Some impressive tombs have been found at various points, but the most evocative is one that stands 1.6 km to the north, just beyond the large reservoir and small theatre of Birketein. **Figure 9.9A**, of the **Tomb of Germanus**, captures something of the splendour of the tomb, the pathos in a grand structure with just three columns standing, and even the stone coffin tumbled out amongst the masonry. Germanus lived in the 2nd century AD and was a centurion in the Roman army, one of several soldiers attested at Jarash.

Arriving at Philadelphia, the ancient traveller would have started to encounter the cemeteries of that city too. The best preserved is not far from the main Roman road from Jarash and halfway between the small Roman town at Yajuz (Fig. 11.5) and Philadelphia. **Qasr Nuweijis (Fig. 9.9B)** is one of several monumental Roman tombs recorded around Amman, though most have suffered badly as the modern city has grown rapidly to engulf them. It is a square building, 14 x 14 m, well-built from carefully cut masonry and with significant architectural decoration. As the photograph shows, it has a parapet around the top and is roofed with a dome supported on internal side arches. Inside are at least two chambers in the corners and recesses in which sarcophagi would have been placed.

The type is seen elsewhere in Jordan — there were other examples around Amman (largely now destroyed by development); certainly some at Jarash — including one thought to have had a tall conical roof. They are usually associated with cities but there is one in an isolated valley at **Khirbat Ain**, 20 km east of Jarash (Fig. 4.1). It was apparently the family tomb of a landowner whose villa must have lain nearby — probably close to the rectangular ancient reservoir visible in the bottom right corner **(Fig. 9.9C)**.

Most large communal tombs tend to be cut into the living rock and survive because they were underground. Little is visible from the air. Conversely, free-standing tombs like these were probably common in antiquity, but have not survived well because they were vulnerable to looters and stone-robbers.

Fig. 9.9A: Jarash (Birketein): Tomb of Germanus (APA99/SL8.10, 14 June 1999, looking northwest)

Fig. 9.9B: Qasr Nuweijis, Amman: looking west over the Roman tomb (APA98/ SL25.30, 17 May 1998)

Fig. 9.9C: Khirbat Ain: Roman tomb in a remote valley (APA00/ SL4.33, 29 August 2000)

Fig. 9.10B: Zeraqun: Roman bridge over the W. Shallalah (APA02.2/ SL16.22, 29 September 2002)

Via Nova Traiana

Rome was rightly famous for its roads. European travellers in the 19th century immediately identified some examples and the network has been expanded much further since then. Roads could be paved where they ran through towns, as at Rabbah (Fig. 9.8A), have a beaten earth surface on a foundation of fieldstones in open countryside (west of Umm el-Jimal) or be simply cleared but generally straight, tracks in areas of desert (north of Qasr el-Azraq: Fig. 13.5). Many roads can be identified as Roman simply from their character — generally straight, well-engineered, paved or with a solid foundation and of a uniform width; many will have guard-posts along their length and often streams will be crossed by a constructed ford, or even a bridge. Many roads are also marked by milestones. Most of these are solid stone columns, about 2 m high and 50–60 cm in diameter; a few are shorter, slimmer columns of black basalt. Some had letters painted on them, but most were probably inscribed with the name of the emperor and, ideally, a distance. At some locations there may be as many as 14 milestones due to generations of repair and rebuilding, with new stones erected each time.

The principal road in Jordan is the famous *Via Nova Traiana*, which some milestones explain extended 'from the borders of Syria as far as the Red Sea'. In fact, it ran from southern Syria, through the provincial capital of Arabia at Bostra, right down past Petra to Aila on the Gulf of Aqaba, a total of *c.* 350 km. In this northern stretch, as far as Amman/ Philadelphia, it was following a new line — or perhaps an old Nabataean route, but after that it followed essentially the line of the ancient King's Highway, which had reached Amman from Jarash and places further north. It was a remarkable piece of engineering. In the desert it can run straight across rolling surfaces; further south, it has to descend in zigzags into a succession of great wadi troughs running into the Dead Sea, then ascend the far side (Figs 2.3, 6.7A and 8.3A). **Figure 9.10A** shows what has long been a well-preserved stretch running west of Umm el-Jimal (Fig. 11.3). The borders and central rib are clearly visible, as well as the fieldstones used for the surface. This is, of course, the sub-structure; the surface was beaten earth on top, but that is long gone. Agriculture is now spreading rapidly in this area and already traces visible 25 years ago are gone and more will soon disappear.

Figure 9.10B shows the bridge over the Wadi esh-Shallalah (Fig. 6.4) about 12 km east of Beit Ras/ Capitolias. At that point the alignment from Beit Ras implies the road would pass about 5 km south of Dera'a (Roman Adraha) on its way to link with the road leading to the provincial capital of Arabia at Bostra, 50 km east of the bridge. The photograph shows the bridge at the bottom of a deep section of the wadi. Part of the abutment where it would have arched over the stream is visible, as are the collapsed remains of the run up to the bridge on the nearest side and the traces of blocks on the hillside opposite. The road itself is not visible. Recent architectural analysis of the remains has concluded it was two storeys high.

Fig. 9.10A: Via Nova Traiana*: southwest of Umm el-Jimal, looking north (APA03/ SL24.32, 30 September, 2004)*

Jarash continued from page 155...

Photo). Leading out of an opening in the top right edge of the piazza, is the start of the 800 m long main street, the Cardo, flanked by magnificent columns and a glittering array of public buildings, as it strikes out for the North Gate in the distance. The original Hellenistic town lay in this southern area, between and on the Zeus hill and Camp Hill (the tree-covered knoll with the museum).

Figure 9.4B includes a long stretch of the Cardo just where it intersects with the North Decumanus, the low light of early morning producing long shadows from each of scores of columns. In the centre of the crossing is the ornamental tetrapylon, roofing the junction. Just to the left lie the ruins of the West Baths, one of two public bath buildings in the town. Dominating the view, even now when only a shadow of their former splendour, are two of the major public buildings of the city. The Temple of Artemis, at the top right, is the major temple of Jarash and one of the largest temples in the ancient world. The temple itself is the striking feature, with columns 1.5 m in diameter and standing 13 m high on a podium 22.6 x 40.1 m. But it sits inside a huge (161 x 121 m) rectangular, colonnaded courtyard, some of whose columns can still be seen buried in the hill slope on the far right. Even that was not all, as the temple complex was the culmination of a long Sacred Way that began on the far side of the river, then ran west through elaborately ornamented features and broad staircases. Part of it can be seen running just above the modern building, where the Department of Antiquities is housed, then across the Cardo and picked up again in the top left with a few columns of the immense Propylaea, a structure that was transformed into a church in the 6th century.

To the right of centre sits the North Theatre, in fact more correctly an Odeon. In front of it runs the North Decumanus and beyond that the recent clearance, underway in this photograph, has identified what may be the forum or *agora* of the city. Just to the right of the theatre is a church, in which a mosaic inscription records its construction in AD 559 by Bishop Isaiah.

10. THE ROMAN ARMY

JORDAN has amongst the best preserved Roman military installations anywhere. In other countries, seemingly well-preserved forts are often quite extensively restored; in Jordan, many of those never excavated still have walls standing several metres high and lack only the roof. The range of sites is immense and most categories of military fortifications are represented in Jordan. The principal force in the early province was the *Legio III Cyrenaica,* about 5,000 citizen soldiers, almost all heavy infantry. It was based in a large (16.8 ha) fortress at Bostra, in southern Syria, but many inscriptions show that numerous detachments were distributed around the rest of the province — some as far away as the Hejaz in Saudi Arabia. The rest of the garrison consisted of regiments recruited from non-citizen provincials. Most were about 500 strong; a few were about 1,000. Their forts were far smaller in size than a legionary fortress but also likely to vary more — cavalry, for example, needed far more space. Then there are the fortlets and towers for detachments outposted from these forts. Of course, the Romans found forts in Jordan already. The Ptolemies, Seleucids and Herodian rulers had all built fortifications. More importantly, the Nabataeans had increasingly modelled their royal army on those of Hellenistic Egypt and Rome. There is growing evidence for Rome's take over of existing Nabataean forts, and in some cases, forts built originally in the Iron Age (Kh. el-Fityan: Fig. 10.5A). Although Rome was present in force from 63 BC, there are very few examples of early Roman forts anywhere in the Near East; but the few we have include excellent examples from Jordan (Fig. 10.4). The Late Roman period — from the late 3rd to the early 7th centuries — is different. There are dozens of forts and again Jordan has some of the best. Equally important, there has been recent large-scale excavation on some of them, helping to provide details of the interiors, their development and the dating. Even where there has been no excavation, Jordan has been fortunate — in the north at least — in the number of sites at which there are dated inscriptions telling us when building occurred (Fig. 10.6).

The locations vary. Initially most Roman soldiers in Jordan were billeted in towns; later they might get their own camps near towns; later still forts were built in the steppe and even the desert. It is the last of these, which are, naturally enough, best preserved. A few still stand in complete isolation (Fig. 10.6); others stimulated settlement around them (Fig. 11.3A) and at others, later still, when the soldiers had gone, civilians moved inside the fort itself (Fig. 11.6). Naturally, the style of forts over such a long timescale changed, as the examples show. The Roman army was also responsible for other features. The best known siege works anywhere in the Roman Empire are at Masada in Israel, but Jordan boasts an exact contemporary example at Machaerus (Fig. 10.1). Temporary camps, that are so common in Britain and northwest Europe, are rare in the Near East but, again, Jordan has some of the few examples (Fig. 10.2). Then there are the towers — hundreds of them, many very ancient but re-used, rebuilt or new in the Roman period (Fig. 10.10). The 4th century AD Roman historian, Ammianus Marcellinus, described Arabia as 'a land producing a rich variety of wares and studded with strong castles and fortresses' (*Hist.* 14.8.13).

The army was responsible for road building — at least the major strategic highways and those linking military posts. Certainly the *Via Nova Traiana* (Fig. 9.10A) was made by soldiers as one papyrus reports. From Jordan we also have a remarkable Latin inscription from the Azraq Oasis (Fig. 13.5) explicitly recording the laying out of a route in the late 3rd century, by detachments from several legions all the way from Bostra, the provincial capital, through Azraq, then down the Wadi Sirhan to Jauf, deep into what is now Saudi Arabia.

Military occupation in the last century of Roman rule is harder to detect archaeologically, but just as Rome took over Nabataean and earlier forts, so too its structures were sometimes put to later use (Fig. 10.3).

Fig. 10.1B: Machaerus: one of Roman siege camps on a ridge around the fortress palace, looking north (APA98/SL30.04, 17 May 1998)

Machaerus (modern Qal'at al-Mishnaqah/ Mukawer)

About 50 km southwest of Amman are a number of steep-sided valleys and hills leading down to the Dead Sea. Amongst them, *c.* 7 km east of the Dead Sea, is a conical hill, famous to New Testament readers as the supposed site of the palace where John the Baptist was executed by Herod Antipas, at the whim of his step-daughter, Salome. The palace had been established by the Jewish Hasmonaean dynasty long before, seized by the Romans in 57 BC, and then developed by Herod the Great in the late 1st century BC as a border fortress against the Nabataeans and palatial safe retreat in his territory east of the River Jordan.

After his death, Herod's kingdom was divided amongst his sons, but a generation later these principalities had mainly been taken over by Rome. Like the much more famous fortress-palace of Masada on the other side of the Dead Sea, a Roman garrison was installed at Machaerus. Both were seized by the rebels in AD 66 when the First Jewish Revolt began and held until at least AD 70, when the governor of Judaea, Lucilius Bassus, led the forces of his province to eliminate pockets of resistance as the revolt came to an end.

We have a description by the contemporary Jewish historian Josephus (*Jewish War* 7.163–216 *passim*, Loeb trans):

He [Lucilius Bassus] next concentrated all the numerous scattered detachments of troops, including the Tenth Legion, having determined to march against Machaerus. ... For the site that is fortified is itself a rocky eminence, rising to so great a height that on that account alone its reduction would be difficult; while nature had further contrived to render it inaccessible. ...

Bassus, after reconnoitring the place on all sides, decided to approach it by filling up the eastern ravine; to this task he now applied himself, labouring to raise with all speed the embankment which was to facilitate the siege.

The siege works were primarily the work of *Legio X Fretensis*, which later also conducted the siege of Masada **(Fig. 10.1B)**. The scale of the siege works is very different to Masada and they were incomplete at the time the defenders capitulated. Nevertheless, a wall of circumvallation, with square towers or buttresses, runs around the adjacent hills. On or close to this wall are 10 or 11 small camps; a large one for the HQ may underlie the modern village of Mukawer.

The photograph **(Fig. 10.1A)** looks down steeply onto the flat-topped hill, with the remains of Herod's palace in the centre. Just beyond, on the ridge leading up to the palace from the west, is the grey mass of the siege ramp. Behind that, at the far end of the ridge, is the grey rectangular outline of a small siege camp. As the view shows, the fortress was well sited for defensibility, but it also offered stunning views out to the west over the Dead Sea and beyond.

The physical remains of the siege are visible today on the surrounding hills to the west, including a ramp to the northeast to alleviate the steep climb for the final assault.

Fig. 10.1A: Machaerus: the fortress palace of Herod the Great overlooking the Dead Sea, looking west (APA98/SL29.34, 17 May 1998)

Temporary Camps

On campaign, the Roman army routinely constructed a fortified camp for itself, even if only for a single night. The traces of these camps are found in the hundreds in northwest Europe, but are rare elsewhere in the Roman Empire. Most of those in Europe were found from the air, which probably explains their rarity in the East where aerial archaeology is seldom possible.

There are a number of temporary camps around the siege circuit at Machaerus and there are the superb, large examples at Masada. But all of those were for siege purposes. The evidence for temporary 'marching camps' is very sparse in this region. A few possibilities are now reported in Jordan, recognized from their distinctive shape and features. In the Early Roman period the temporary camp was commonly rectangular, with the unique rounded corners of the Roman military structure — the so-called playing-card shape.

At Azamia on the flat plain, just north of the Dead Sea and about 10 km west of Mt Nebo, is a most unusual site **(Fig. 10.2A).** Seen on air photographs it strikes a Roman archaeologist immediately as a Roman temporary camp: a rectangle of *c.* 110 x 75 m, 0.825 ha, with possible rounding of the corners. The size is comparable to Camps A and C at Masada and sufficient to house perhaps 1,000 men. Inside is a large square reservoir. Examination on the ground revealed rounded corners and possible entrances one third of the way along the longer sides — both are features of Roman camps. The date of construction is unknown. It might belong to the campaigns of the First Jewish War (AD 66–*c.* 74) or to Roman campaigns against the Nabataeans; perhaps even to the campaign of annexation in AD 106.

The second example **(Fig. 10.2B)**, is in the very different environment, encountered far to the southeast, on the way out to the Al-Jafr Oasis — a low rolling, chert-covered landscape, criss-crossed by seasonal water courses. Few sites are found here, but beside the Wadi Abu Safut is this unexpected new discovery. It is large, *c.* 200 x 130m, 2.6 ha, big enough to accommodate *c.* 3,000 men, if indeed, it is a Roman camp.

Fig. 10.2A: Azaima: looking southwest over the rectangular outline of the Roman camp towards the Dead Sea (APA98/ SL28.1, 17 May 1998)

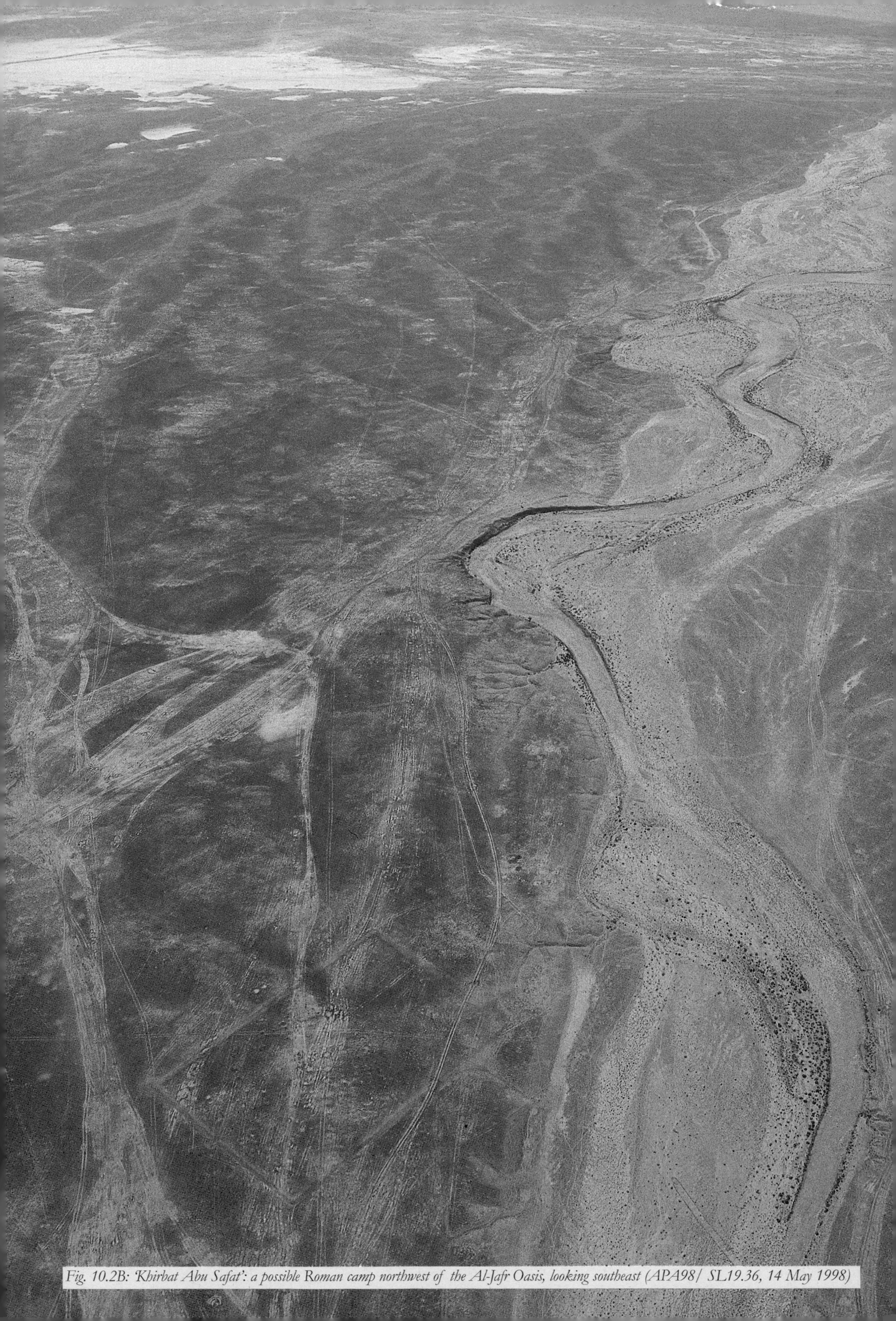

Fig. 10.2B: 'Khirbat Abu Safat': a possible Roman camp northwest of the Al-Jafr Oasis, looking southeast (APA98/ SL19.36, 14 May 1998)

Fig. 10.3A: Qasr el-Hallabat. Looking southwest (APA97/SL6.05, 27 May 1997)

Qasr el-Hallabat

This remarkable ruin lies *c.* 45 km northeast of Amman **(Fig. 10.3A)**. It is one of a series of forts in a large area east of the *Via Nova Traiana* — 27 km east in this case — which dominate an area between the Roman highway and the Azraq Oasis some 55 km away. It lies at a junction of two vertical environmental zones, the steppe lands of the west, and the desert. More than that, it lies where two lateral sub-zones meet — the Basalt Desert of the north and the Chert Desert to the south. The steppe could be extensively settled in the right conditions; the Basalt Desert was extensively used by nomads who left their mark; the Chert Desert is sparsely marked by human traces.

The site is a multi-period one. Pottery and an inscription reveal Nabataean settlement. Next came a Roman military structure — probably a small square fortlet, then a larger fort to which towers were subsequently added. Finally, the fort was converted to an Umayyad country mansion, with plastered walls, elaborate mosaic floors with gold leaf decoration, a mosque, a bathhouse 3 km away, an irrigated 'garden' nearby and houses scattered all around.

Figure 10.3A is a panorama looking southwest. The fort stands in a commanding position on a small outcrop, with extensive views across the plains from northwest to southeast. In the distance beyond the fort is the outline of a large irregular reservoir (*c.* 80 x 80 m) and there are a score of cisterns scattered around the site. In the foreground is one of a dozen houses, probably Umayyad in date. Dominating everything is the fort and the small Umayyad mosque to its left.

In **Figure 10.3B** we can see the fort in detail — *c.* 38 m square, 0.13 ha, with projecting corner towers. Most of the stone was a honey-coloured limestone, but black basalt was later used extensively in the internal remodelling of the Umayyad period. Here we are looking northwest. The main entrance is on the top right into a vestibule area, then under an arch to the courtyard. The staircase shows that at least some of the rooms round the courtyard were two storeyed. An inscription built into the wall nearby, records construction in AD 529. However, a second inscription, now at the old RAF station at Marka (Fig. 14.8A), records building work in *c.* AD 212 and calls the fort *castellum novum,* the 'New Fort'. That may imply an even earlier fort. In fact, in the bottom left corner, the unexcavated area is a small enclosure 17.5 m square which may be Nabataean or Roman. Next would come the large square fort encapsulating the earlier. Finally, the walls were raised in height, second storeys added to the rooms and three-storeyed towers inserted at the corners. There are dozens of inscriptions on the site, mainly re-used in walls, and principally part of a large Greek edict of the late 5th/ early 6th century. Found nearby was a late 3rd century milestone.

Fig. 10.3B: Qasr el-Hallabat. looking northwest (APA97/SL6.26, 27 May 1997)

Fig. 10.4B: Humayma: detail of the Roman fort, looking southwest (APA98/ SL40.29, 20 May 1998)

Humayma

Details of the Roman annexation of the Nabataean kingdom are scarce and how the new province was organized during the next century is almost unknown. Now, however, we have the exciting results of excavation from this important fort.

Humayma lies beside the great Roman highway, the *Via Nova Traiana,* halfway between Petra and Aqaba on the Red Sea. The road has just descended the steep scarp of the Shera'a mountain range and started across the flat desert of the northern Hisma. At this point the desert meets a lateral mountain range and forms a pocket. Here a settlement was founded by the Nabataean king, Aretas III (85–62 BC), expanded still further in the Roman period. This was the town from which the Abassid family (AD 690–750), which was to displace the Umayyad dynasty (Ch. 4), came. It is now commonly agreed that Humayma is the *Hauara* of the ancient documents — the 'White Place'. In particular, a Late Roman document of about AD 400, reported Hauara as the base of *Equites sagittarii indigenae* — a regiment of 'Native Horse Archers'.

At its fullest extent it was a town of some 10 ha, with buildings scattered across a wide area. Outstanding is the large rectangular structure, identified as a fort and now known from excavation to be that rarity in the Middle East, an early Roman imperial fort. Several seasons of excavation have made it one of the best-known military sites in Jordan.

The photograph **(Fig. 10.4A)** shows the dramatic location very well — the hills creating the bay in which the town lies, and the trough of the great Wadi Araba beyond. The town is on the centre left. Dominating the centre of the photograph is the grey outline of the large fort. It is an almost perfect rectangle, 700 x 500 Roman feet (206.32 x 148.3 m, 3.05 ha) **(Fig. 10.4B).** There are gates in the centres of the north and south walls and also — as was common — off-centre in the east and west. Especially important for the study of military architecture in the East is the presence of projecting, square towers all around — one on each corner and 20 more at intervals along the walls. Until recently, this was thought to be a design feature introduced in the 3rd century. Here, however, the excavator has dated the first Roman fort to the annexation period, in or soon after AD 106.

Inside the North Gate is a *Principia*, the HQ building, with a typical colonnaded courtyard and pitched roof with terracotta tiles. The earliest rooms were plastered, with the upper half covered in elaborate polychrome frescoes. Excavation elsewhere in the fort recovered 'Buckles, three-bladed arrow heads, spear points and butts, sections of scale armour, hobnails for boots, and the cheekpiece of an iron helmet, with fragments of leather still adhering to its inside surface'. Food refuse included, not just the expected sheep and goat bones, but those of pigs and chickens too; there are also oyster shells — presumably brought from the Red Sea, *c.* 45 km to the south.

As elsewhere in Jordan the water supply was probably originally Nabataean. A ground level aqueduct has now been traced from the springs on the scarp to the north. This emptied into a large rectangular reservoir, just southwest of where the fort was later constructed. When the fort was laid out, a spur was led off from the aqueduct to fill a second reservoir in the top right corner of the fort, which and could hold *c.* 1,275 cu metres.

The excavator interprets Phase I from soon after AD 106 to the late 3rd century; Phase II belongs to the 4th century and ended in a slow decline.

Fig. 10.4A: Humayma: looking southwest over the town of Hauara in a bay of the Hisma Desert. In the centre is the rectangular outline of the Roman fort (APA98/SL40.23, 20 May 1998)

Fig. 10.5B: El-Lejjun: Late Roman legionary fortress, looking northwest (APA01/SL10.02, 3 October 2001)

El-Lejjun

Lejjun is located about 15 km east of Kerak (Fig. 13.1) and has been a focal point for military activity for centuries. It lies on the edge of the steppe and desert, just at a point where springs turn a small valley into a fertile garden zone. The modern name, attested since the 19th century, reflects the belief that this was a camp for a Roman legion.

The place has attracted settlement and military attention in various periods, as graphically shown in the striking panorama of **Figure 10.5A**. In the centre of the landscape, on the plateau, is a large irregular Bronze Age fortress. On the edge of a scarp on the right, is a square late Iron Age fort re-used in Roman times (Kh. el-Fityan). To the left, two parallel rows of 8 buildings are the Ottoman barracks. Finally, in the bottom left is the Roman fortress. (There are also five 19th century watermills in the wadi; cf. Fig. 14.)

The second photograph **(Fig. 10.5B)** shows the fortress in detail, including the traces of modern excavation. Along with the other Late Roman fortress at Udruh, Lejjun is one of the two largest purely military structures in Jordan. Despite extensive removal of stone for re-use, the site remains remarkably well preserved and has impressed writers from the 19th century onwards. The extensive modern excavations have made it the best-known and probably most important Roman military site in Jordan.

The fortress is a rectangle, *c.* 247 x 190 m, *c.* 4.7 ha, with massive walls: *c.* 2.5 m thick, standing perhaps 5–6 m high. There are 24 massive towers, U-shaped (on the walls) and semi-circular (at the corners), probably two storeys high and projecting up to 11 m. A road between the south (centre left) and north (centre right) gates (*Via Principalis*) divides the interior in two and another, with colonnades, from the east gate (*Via Praetoria*) (bottom right) meets it at right angles, in the typical T-pattern of so many Roman forts. Above the junction lies a *Principia,* the HQ building. The commonest buildings are the barrack blocks, whose layout could be seen even before excavation. In fact, we now know that there were two phases of development inside. The Phase 1 barracks (*c.* AD 300) consisted of 8 long blocks, each with 18 pairs of rooms, a total of 144 pairs, each room *c.* 5.1 x 5 m. The roofs were apparently tiled. Phase 2 is dated to soon after AD 363 and resulted in major changes to the barracks.

Later work included the construction of a church *c.* AD 500. Outside the walls were extensive traces of settlement, including a *Mansio*, an inn.

Few Early Roman legionary fortresses are known anywhere in the East and none has been excavated. Here we have a well-preserved Late Roman legionary fortress when legions had become much smaller. The garrison is estimated to have been *c.* 2,000 men in Phase 1 and *c.* 1,000 in Phase 2 compared with the *c.* 20 ha needed for the *c.* 5,000 men of an Early Roman legion. The best guess is that its garrison was the one named in the Late Roman army list of *c.* AD 400, the *Notitia Dignitatum*: the '*Legion IV Martia, at Betthorus*'.

Fig. 10.5A: El-Lejjun: Late Roman legionary fortress, Ottoman barracks and Bronze Age hill-fort (APA02.2/SL22.36, 30 September 2002)

Fig. 10.7B: Da'ajaniya: a vertical view of the Late Roman fort of c. AD 300 (APA98/SL20.12, 14 May 1998)

Da'ajaniya

This Roman fort lies on the edge of the steppe, some 40 km northeast of Petra; the *Via Nova Traiana* is *c.* 12 km to the west. It is well preserved, the circuit wall, 2.5 m thick, still stands 3–4 m high. Large square towers, 8 m square, straddle each corner, with others set at intervals along the walls and flanking the gate in the middle of the east wall. As **Figure 10.7A** shows, the place is a striking one; the black of the basalt building material stands out starkly against the yellow-orange surroundings. The region is arid, but considerable quantities of water passed along the wadis seasonally and, as at Qasr Bshir (Fig. 10.6) far to the north, water was diverted into a large reservoir. Test excavation has dated construction to *c.* AD 300.

The vertical view **(Fig. 10.7B)** readily shows the entire plan in detail. It is almost a perfect square, and the size, 100 x 100 m, 1 ha, is very similar to that of several other Roman forts of this same date in Jordan (e.g. Umm el-Jimal: Fig. 11.3A). All around the inner face of the curtain wall are 60 rooms that are conventionally shown as long rectangles, perhaps stables for horses. However, the photograph shows that those on the north side (right), at least, are divided into pairs of square rooms. Some may have been two storeys. In the middle, suites of square rooms are grouped in short barracks blocks, enough for some 200 to 300 soldiers. In the middle of the north range (right), a different layout of rooms suggests that this is the *Principia,* the HQ building. One estimate suggests space for as many as *c.* 500 soldiers plus animals.

Some water was stored in the cistern visible at the western end (top) of the main east–west street. More important, however, was the reservoir (bottom centre **Fig 10.7A**).

The location suggests a unit to patrol and police the steppe and protect the settlements of the Jebel Da'ajaniya area to the west (the Khatt Shebib runs through that area: Fig. 8.7). The reservoir — now brought back into use for beduins — suggests provision for large numbers of animals. Da'ajaniya may have been a mustering point for nomads and herders, comparable, perhaps, to what has been suggested for Qasr Bshir.

Fig. 10.7A: Da'ajaniya: a Late Roman fort of c. AD 300. Looking northwest (APA98/SL20.4, 14 May 1998)

Fig. 10.8A: Qasr el-Aseikhim: a small Roman outpost fort and prehistoric enclosure, looking southwest (APA97/SL4.17, 27 May 1997)

Fig. 10.8B: Qasr el-Aseikhim: the Roman fort, looking northwest (APA97/ SL4.33, 27 May 1997)

Qasr Aseikhim

The site is 13.5 km northeast of the pools of Azraq Duruz in the Azraq Oasis. Difficulty of access has left Aseikhim relatively unexplored, but a few of the more intrepid travellers of a century ago made it there — Gertrude Bell visited on 31 December 1913. Situated on the peak of a volcanic hill still capped with lava, this site enjoys one of the most spectacular locations of any Roman fort as **Figure 10.8A** shows. From the summit one can see for long distances in every direction, including back over the Azraq Oasis and the Roman road that ran to it.

There are several components. The fort is constructed inside an earlier circuit wall in the shape of a large teardrop. A further wall, to the left of this in the foreground, and showing more faintly seems to be an annexe to it. The usual interpretation sees this as 'prehistoric', but little is known about it. Just to the right and below the summit, is the square outline of a dried out reservoir, formed by a dam wall. On the left, behind the summit, is an area of stone heaps, of a type usually associated with land clearance for agriculture. In the bottom right corner, just above the track made recently by a bulldozer, are the jumbled walls of some structures.

The Roman fort **(Fig. 10.8B)** occupies the very summit. Walls still stand over 3 m high. Some rooms still have arches for roofs and some of their corbelling in place. The door on the south gives onto a vestibule, leading into a small courtyard around which single-storeyed rooms are arranged symmetrically about an axis through this doorway. Stairs lead to the roof.

There has been no excavation, and no inscriptions or coins have been found, but surface pottery gives some clues. One suggestion is of a possible Nabataean occupation, followed in the Roman period by a fort. That was probably short-lived, but there may have been some occupation in the mid-6th into the 7th centuries. Plans are in train to develop this site and surrounding area as an achaeological park.

Fig. 10.9B: Khirbat el-Khalde: vertical view of the fortified Roman road station (APA98/SL42.19, 21 May 1998)

Khirbat el-Khalde

Between Humayma and the Red Sea port of Aqaba, much of the route passes along the Wadi Yitm. It is a narrow valley with high rugged mountains on either side, forcing all traffic to follow either this route or the stifling and largely waterless Wadi Araba to the west. A Roman map records that at 23 Roman miles south of Humayma (Fig. 10.3) there is a place called *Praesidium*, the ancient term for a police post on a road. The army list of *c.* AD 400 has the entry for this part of Jordan — '*The Cohors IV Phrygum, at Praesidium*'.

The place on the map coincides with where the Wadi Yitm opens out into a broader bay, 2–3 km wide, and where there is a spring on the slope on the east. As **Figure 10.9A** shows, the wadi is arid and interrupted by rocky outcrops. It also shows graphically just how important the route is — the Roman road ran through here, the early modern unsurfaced road is in the bottom right corner, the railway comes next, then the recent motor road and finally the current highway. For at least 2,000 years everyone has had to come this way.

The prominent ruins are on the east side of the valley, *c.* 800 m northwest of the spring. The detailed photograph **(Fig. 10.9B)** shows two rectangular structures. The fort is the larger rectangular enclosure, 49.5 x 32 m, with an entrance on the north (left) and projecting towers at each corner, *c.* 6 m square. Inside the enclosure there are rooms all around built against the walls. The resulting courtyard is divided into unequal parts by a range of rooms, running north to south and apparently consisting of pairs of rooms on either side of a central wall. In the centre of the larger courtyard is a square reservoir fed by a channel coming from the top of the photograph, to run under the centre of the enclosure wall. The smaller courtyard included a bath suite, hypocaust pillars for which have been exposed. A bath building at a military site is a relative rarity in the Middle East.

About 50 m to the south of the fort, is what seems to be a caravanserai, *c.* 32 x 22 m. It is oriented on the fort, uses masonry similar to it and seems contemporary. The entrance is in the north wall. It leads into a small courtyard, surrounded by rooms, roughly built against the enclosure wall all around.

Not visible is the spring and long channel from it to the fort, or the group of cisterns to the northwest of the fort.

The fort seems to have three phases of construction; there is Nabataean and Roman pottery and several late 3rd/ 4th century Roman coins. Milestones of AD 112 have been found on the *Via Nova Traiana*, a short distance north of Khalde, others show rebuilding in AD 293–305 and 307–308.

A Nabataean military post seems likely at Khalde and that may be the origin of the caravanserai as well. It was certainly a Roman fort at a key point on a route and the fort, at least, underwent a minimum of two later modifications. Indeed, it may originally have been a small square fort, to which an annexe was added on the west.

Fig. 10.9A: Khirbat el-Khalde: a fortified Roman road station, looking northwest (APA98/SL42.18, 21 May 1998)

Fig. 10.10A: Qasr Burqu: the late Roman tower surrounded by later Islamic residence, looking west (APA98/ SL32.15, 18 May 1998)

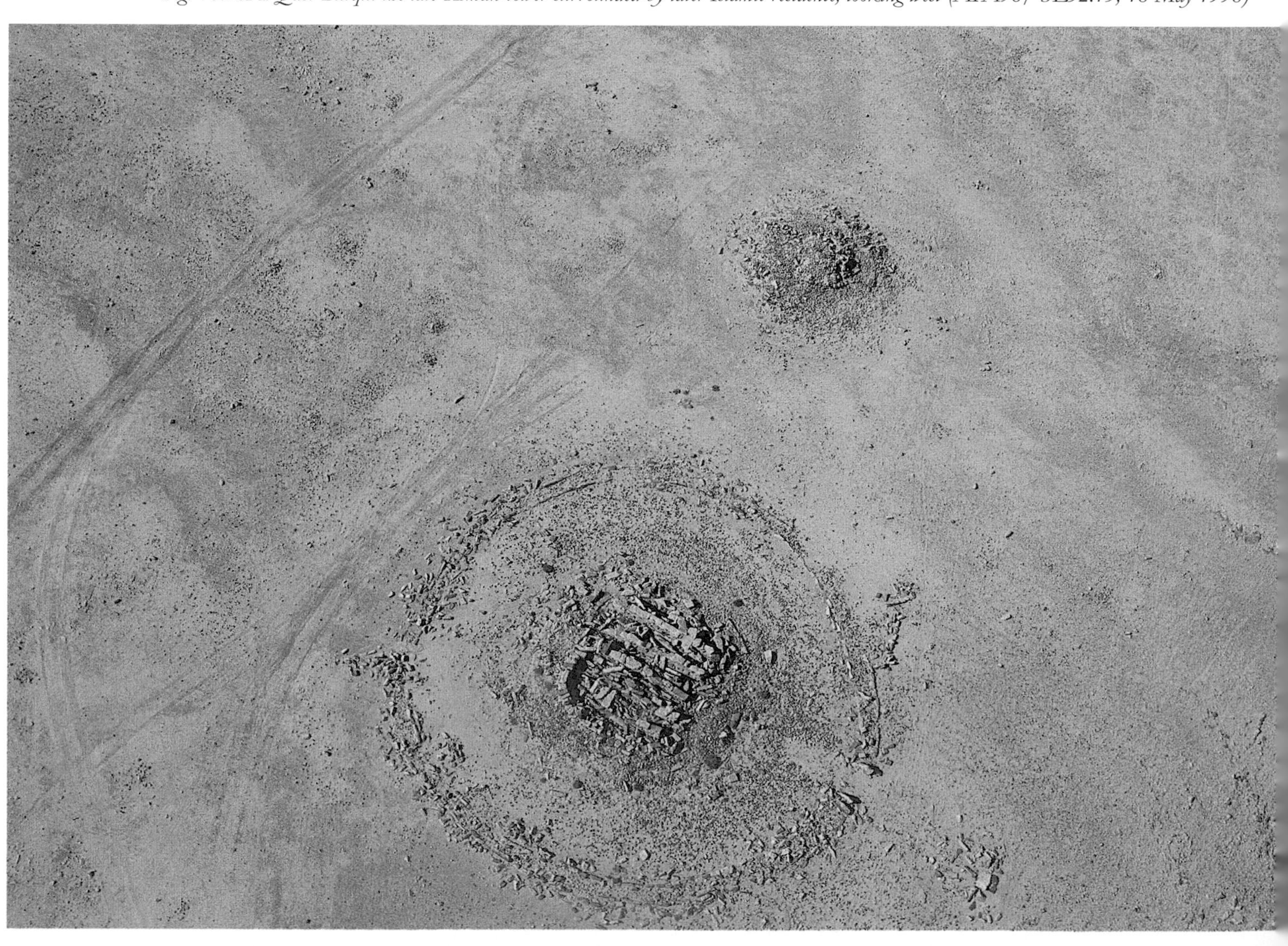

Fig. 10.10C: Qasr Abu Rukbah: Roman tower south of El-Lejjun, looking northeast (APA98/SL16.35, 15 May 1998)

Towers

Jordan is littered with towers — several hundred at least, scattered over the hills and it often seems from the air as if every other hilltop is marked by a tower. In fact, in some places while photographing one tower, we discovered that two or more others were visible. Few have been explored in detail and dates are often unknown. It is clear that many go back at least to the Bronze and Iron Age and in several instances towers may have been re-used and repaired on several occasions over long periods.

Their purpose varied. Some could be simple watch towers on the approach to settlements, others were guarding watering points and still others were built along routes to police travellers. **Figure 10.10A** is the tower of Qasr Burqu 205 kms northeast of Amman, far out in the Basalt Desert. It is probably Late Roman in date, but surrounded by an Islamic desert residence, which made use of it. In this case it watches over a lake, created by a dam, and over a remote desert route.

South of Amman there are scores of towers in the area near the Wadi Mujib. **Figure 10.10B** is an example from between Qasr Bshir (Fig. 10.6) and Lejjun (Fig. 10.5). In this case the square tower is set inside a near perfect circular enclosure. Then there is Qasr Abu Rukbah (**Fig. 10.10C),** 14 km south of the fortress of Lejjun, a good example showing the quality of preservation, the locations and the loneliness of many such places. It is *c.* 10.5 m square, with walls *c.* 1.3 m thick. Test-excavation here has suggested it was originally a Roman construction.

Fig. 10.10B: an unnamed tower between Qasr Bshir and El-Lejjun, near vertical (APA01/SL8.23, 2 October 2001)

11. CHRISTIAN ROMAN JORDAN

LATE Roman Jordan is a different world from the Hellenistic and early Roman periods. The Roman world was changing already in the 2nd century AD, but Constantine's adoption of Christianity in the early 4th century brought more and new changes. These changes can be seen in the landscape and in the new religious architecture of the period. Christians no longer needed to hide their meetings; now, indeed, their congregations were given buildings sponsored by the state. A huge building programme began everywhere, not least in the Holy Land itself, until then rather a neglected backwater, but now made a focal point of religious devotion.

Some pagan temples were converted for Christian use, or their building stone re-used, as in Jerusalem with the great Hadrianic pagan temples. But new buildings, designed for the needs of the new religion, soon appeared in large numbers. Churches, monasteries and convents came to dominate the urban landscape. It is remarkable how even quite small towns (Figs 11.3–11.5), or even just large villages, constructed multiple churches, often quite large, and increasingly provided with impressive mosaic floors. But they also appear in this region — the Holy Land — at places associated with significant figures in Biblical history and the founding of the religion. Mt Nebo (Fig. 11.1A), from which Moses was reputedly shown the Promised Land is one, another is the recently discovered Baptism site on the east bank of the Jordan. Here the needs were distinct. The sacred buildings had to provide for pilgrims in an external precinct, and ancillary buildings (*xenodochia*) were needed for sheltering and feeding them. Along the routes to such popular pilgrimage places, churches came to provide hospitality for travellers.

Most churches are aisled buildings — the basilical style consisting of a central nave, with colonnades along either side, separating off two aisles. The nave itself ends in an apse and sometimes the aisles do as well. Mosaics are often highly elaborate and it became common to include a text as part of the mosaic, setting out the dedication and the name of the dedicant — usually the local bishop. Consequently, the churches can sometimes be precisely dated by the mosaic. In some instances new mosaics were laid like carpets, one on top of the other. Church mosaics include not just the world famous Madaba Map mosaic — part of a map of the Holy Land with places depicted and labelled — but also those from the church at Mt Nebo. And now we have the splendid mosaics from Umm er-Resas, one depicting and naming a dozen towns and cities of the region (Fig. 11.6)

The wealth and vigour so evident in the decoration of the churches of Jordan is the counterpart to another development. Ground surveys have revealed a continuing rise in the number of sites of all kinds in this period. After the growth in the size and elaboration of cities and growing number of sites in the Early Roman period, it is interesting to see the trend continue strongly. It is especially true of the marginal areas. In an earlier chapter several forts were illustrated of the period *c.* AD 300 and later. Many such forts are located in the steppe or out into the desert beyond. Although we do not know the details of the process, what is clear is that increased security is paralleled by the extensive and intensive settlement of the steppe and even of pockets of cultivatable land in the Basalt Desert. Ground surveys have revealed traces of Nabataean or still earlier settlement at some of these places, but the fullest flourishing belongs to this Late Roman period and continues strongly in the Umayyad period that follows (Fig. 11.3).

Traces of this new dense settlement can be seen throughout Jordan, in almost every modern village and quite often in places where only the ancient village exists to this day. The best examples come from the northeast however, in the steppe east of the Decapolis and the belt of fertile soils that extends eastwards along both sides of the modern frontier with Syria, in what is known as the Southern Hauran. In Syria itself is the provincial capital, the important city and legionary base of Bostra. All around, however, were the remarkable small towns and villages living off the fertile soils they could now fully cultivate. Security allowed them to undertake the labour-intensive clearance of boulders off the surface and the channelling of water from the lower rainfall into cisterns and reservoirs. Characteristic of this steppe area are the water collection and storage facilities. Thousands of cisterns, scores of large open reservoirs and dozens of channels have been recorded. In places one can still see fossilized field systems — field boundaries and hillside terracing. These features are notoriously difficult to date, but the best guess is that as they are usually in marginal areas. They belong to the period when settlement was at its most extensive and the margins were developed.

Fig. 11.2B: Abila: the restored 7th century AD basilica on Umm el-Amad, looking north (APA98/SL44.19, 21 May 1998)

Abila (modern Qweilbeh)

Twenty kilometres east of Gadara (Fig. 9.6A) lies another Decapolis city, ancient Abila. It was evidently a significant city though it remained little known until major excavations began in 1980. The location is an attractive one with a stream, springs and rich agricultural lands. There are traces of settlement at and around the town site from at least the Neolithic through to the Ottoman period. Not surprisingly, it is the remains of the Bronze Age and the long millennium from Hellenistic to Umayyad times that are the most extensive and notable. Overall the remains have been traced over an area of about 1,500 (NS) x 750 m (EW) (112.5 ha) which the excavator thought might be home to an urban community of *c.* 7–8,000 people. Although there are significant traces in the town and cemeteries of the Hellenistic and, even more, the Early Roman period, the most visible excavated structures are Late Roman churches.

Figure 11.2A is looking southwest over the civic centre in the centre. The bowl of the theatre, later extensively looted of its stone, as well as being re-used for a major Umayyad building, is visible in the facing hill slope just above the road in the centre. In the foreground is the first of several churches. A second church lies on the low ground, just to the left of the theatre and a third on Tell Abila, just off the photograph to the right. In the distance towards the top of the photograph is the 7th century large basilica. It is a building, 20 x 41 m, with 6 columns across an entrance porch and 24 columns in two rows behind, leading to a triple apse. As the detailed photograph shows (**Fig. 11.2B**), there are traces of other buildings beside it and indeed beyond.

Fig. 11.2A: Abila: looking southwest across the civic centre, theatre and restored basilica on Umm el-Amad (APA98/SL44.8, 21 May 1998)

Fig. 11.5B: Yajuz: looking northeast across the valley immediately below Yajuz (APA98/SL26.03, 17 May 1998)

Yajuz

Eleven kilometres north of Amman, on the Roman road to Gerasa, one crosses a small east–west valley. Milestones have been found here and further north on this road. On the north slope are the buried ruins of a substantial settlement — at 20 ha, probably a small town. Today it is only 4 km from the nearest suburbs of Amman and the valley itself is being developed rapidly. Part of the site has been damaged and, as **Figure 11.5A** shows, buildings are beginning to encroach. The threat to this important place is worrying. Excavations have already revealed Late Roman churches, an industrial area, wine presses and tombs. Although the mosaics are poorly preserved they are abundant and the place seems to have been prosperous: presumably one of a scatter of such villages around the classical city of Philadelphia (Amman). Excavation has now shown that settlement continued well into the Abassid period.

The second photograph **(Fig. 11.5B)** is a view looking southeast from above Yajuz. The lush fertile valley explains the attraction of the place. There is terracing on the far slope and in medieval and Ottoman times the new settlement in the valley was where the present village now stands.

Fig. 11.5A: Yajuz: looking northwest across the churches and Late Roman buildings of the village (APA98/SL25.35, 17 May 1998)

Fig. 11.7B: El-Mureigha: looking east over the 'fort' and some of its surrounding earthworks (APA98/SL16.28, 14 May 1998)

El-Mureigha

Most of the settlements of Late Roman Jordan were neither cities nor important towns like Madaba, nor even such small towns as Umm el-Jimal, Hayyan al-Mashrif and Yajuz (Figs 11.3, 11.4 and 11.5). In the next pages we shall look at some of the villages and farms. There are still other places that defy any easy definition, but were probably numerous. El-Mureigha is one of those.

The site lies 11 km southeast of Kerak, at a natural crossroads on the fertile plain of central Moab **(Fig. 11.7A).** It lies on the highest point of a ridge, overlooking the plain all around and the trade routes that intersected nearby. Surface exploration has found pottery in abundance from several periods and it is apparent that there was settlement at this place from at least the Early Bronze Age. All commentators, however, seem agreed that the first major occupation was probably Nabataean. Without excavation we cannot be sure of dates. Commentators have insisted, however, that the walled area is Late Roman and Umayyad, and one has even called it a 'city' and referred to a street. Certainly it is the walled area that catches the eye. It measures *c.* 90 x 105 m, *c.* 1 ha, too small for a 'city'. However, there is an extension on the southeast corner (nearest the viewer in Fig. 11.7A) and there are traces of buildings outside this walled area. It is perhaps more likely that this was a fort — whether Nabataean or Roman — which was later taken over and became a small town. The size is very similar to that of forts of *c.* AD 300 (eg Figs 10.7; 11.3). As at the much larger Umm er-Resas (Fig. 11.6) there is evidence of a church inside the walls. A recent scholar noted that a large Late Roman cemetery on the east-southeast side was being systematically looted.

Figure 11.7B shows the 'fort' in detail. The regular layout of buildings inside may be late in date but overlying earlier military ones. Traces can be seen too, of projecting towers at the corners and on the walls. The main entrance is in the middle of the wall on the left. At the right, there is a smaller square enclosure of *c.* 45 x 40 m attached to the south wall of the fort.

Both photographs show extensive traces of earthworks all around and it is likely a good deal is buried here. Certainly, there must have been an elaborate system for collecting and preserving water, perhaps by a dam on the neighbouring wadi.

Fig. 11.7A: El-Mureigha: looking north over the site and its surrounding fertile plain (APA98/SL16.25, 14 May 1998)

Fig. 11.8A: Tahuna: panoramic view looking southeast over the town, hydraulic facilities and encircling wall (APA00/SL7.26 (RHB), 14 September 200

Tahuna

Despite its great extent, almost nothing is known of this important site. It lies in southern Jordan *c.* 20 km to the east-southeast of Petra and just south of the main road to Ma'an. It is an area with numerous sites, not least of the Roman period. The Late Roman legionary fortress and town of Udruh is 12 km to the northwest and smaller sites are strewn across the surrounding hills. Particularly notable are the extensive water collection facilities, including the system of chain wells known as *qanats* or *foggara* (cf. Fig. 12.2A). Several chains of these are found between Udruh and Tahuna, although these are generally thought to be later than the Islamic conquest.

Visitors have commented on the prominent large square reservoir (centre Fig. 11.8A), they have also reported a dam across the wadi, a church and 'Castellum'. A wall has been traced round part of the site for 4 km and is said to be *c.* 2.5 m high. However, much of the site is buried and scarcely intelligible at ground level. The surface pottery is said to be 'Byzantine' (= Late Roman).

The aerial view gives shape, definition and further detail. The panoramic view **(Fig. 11.8A)** encompasses most of the site. Circling round the top, in an inverted U-shape, can be seen the enclosure wall: it follows a meandering course on the left, turns through a wide curve (top), then runs relatively straight (top right), before turning again into the third stretch (bottom right). In the upper part of this enclosure can be seen the dark line, of what may be, a buried channel leading towards a rectangular garden. In the centre of the photograph is a large square reservoir. The traces of buildings are concentrated towards the bottom.

Fig. 11.8B: Tahuna: detail of the settlement (APA98/SL19.6, 14 May 1998)

In the detailed view **(Fig. 11.8B)**, amongst a scatter of smaller rectilinear buildings, there is a large square structure with internal rooms against the walls — a residence, caravanserai or fort. Further out still are traces of fields and an aqueduct channel. A kilometre to the west, a chain of wells runs for several hundred metres westwards.

The overall impression is of a farming community and a residence or fort surrounded by settlement. There are widespread traces of water collection, storage and distribution. It is in this area that the church historian Eusebius, writing *c.* AD 293, places 'Theman', a 'village' with a garrison, 15 (or in the Latin translation, 5) Roman miles from Petra and another garrison at 'Carcaria', which he says is one days' journey from Petra.

Fig. 11.9B: Ruins of three villages northwest of Ras en-Naqb. Looking northeast (APA98/ SL40.18, 20 May 1998)

Nakhl and Late Roman Villages

The Roman Near East has been called a 'world of villages'. This is especially true of the Late Roman period, when villages are common and the churches that marked them were amongst the latest buildings erected and are still prominent amongst the ruins.

This site has long been regarded as one of the larger and more striking ruined villages on the central Moabite plateau. The ruins have not been built over, or at least not recently **(Fig. 11.9A)**. Surface examination, some excavation and an examination of written records, indicates that there has been settlement of some kind at the site since the Early Bronze Age and that it continued in every major period through to Ottoman times. The major occupation periods, as so often, are from the Nabataean to Early Islamic periods.

The place is surrounded by extensive arable land, and the result of protracted settlement was to create ruins extending over an irregular area of about 500 x 300 m, *c.* 15 ha. As the plate shows, however, the ruins are not continuous. On the northeast side there are the ruins of what has been identified as a Nabataean temple, but nearby are those of a church. Also visible are the outlines of numerous rectilinear buildings, divided into rooms — undoubtedly houses, but undated. Cutting into the centre of the village is a series of parallel earthworks. Such cross wadi walls are common in the region as a method for controlling water and creating fields. In this case, they may be part of an irrigated 'garden close', which was later surrounded by the growth of the settlement.

Numerous sites of this type are to be found throughout the region, some (as here) unoccupied, others partly overlain, some largely hidden beneath modern villages or towns. There are few modern villages in Jordan which do not show traces of earlier occupation, often of the 'Roman' period. The second photograph **(Fig. 11.9B)** illustrates the point well. Here, just north and northwest of Ras en-Naqb, the plateau is strewn with the ruins of deserted villages. In this instance, three are visible as grey ruins amongst the gold of the cereal fields, at the left centre, centre foreground and top right, just along the lower edge of the modern highway. No dates are known, but we may be confident that whatever other period is represented, the Late Roman will be amongst them, in some, if not all cases.

Fig. 11.9A: Nakhl: looking northwest over the ruins of the village (APA98/ SL37.12, 20 May 1998)

Fig. 11.10B: Faynan: detail of the settlement, looking north (APA98/SL38.19, 20 May 1998)

Faynan

The Wadi Araba stretching south from the Dead Sea, as the continuation of the Rift Valley, is studded with archaeological sites. On the northeast side, 40 km north of Petra lies Faynan. It is the centre of an area encompassing about 250 mines and hundreds of thousands of tons of slag, over a radius of 15+ km, from millennia of copper extraction (cf. Fig. 7.10). Activity was so intense that the soils over a large area remain seriously contaminated to this day. As early as the 19th century, German scholars were active in the region and it is currently under survey and excavation by British archaeologists.

In its final major phase of occupation it was called Phaino and was worked from the 1st century BC to the 5th century AD. The greatest concentration however, came after the Roman annexation of AD 106, when it probably became a state-controlled activity, exploiting the minerals and farming the land intensively. In the time of the Late Roman church historian Eusebius (late 3rd/ early 4th centuries AD), it was a settlement and a copper-working site, a terrible place to which Christians were condemned to labour and a number were martyred.

Faynan itself is a large and multifaceted site, stretching some 5 km along the wadi. In this panorama **(Fig. 11.10A)**, the site is illuminated by a glaring, late-morning sun, which rakes light along parts of the complex of ancient structures and makes even the dry wadi look as if it contains water. Several components are picked up in this low oblique view looking east. Beginning west of the settlement, is an extensive area of some 900 ancient fields that run in a strip up to a kilometre wide, for almost four kilometres ending just in the right foreground of this photograph. The small, irregularly shaped fields were irrigated by water, channelled off the neighbouring slopes. There is also a small area of settlement here, beyond which lie dark heaps of copper slag. Beyond the tributary, on the right, is a second large area of settlement and ancient cemeteries. The principal settlement of Khirbat Faynan sits on a rise on the north bank (at left).

Figure 11.10B shows the settlement in detail. In the centre is the clear shape of a large square structure, dominating the summit of the hill. On the lower slopes all around is a dense concentration of dozens of rectilinear buildings. These thin out into a series of much more isolated buildings along the lower ground around the hill.

The Christian sources imply that there was a significant military presence. As yet though, no fort has been traced, unless it is the middle of the settlement.

Fig. 11.10A: Faynan: panorama looking east over part of the field system, the copper-working area and the settlement (APA98/SL38.22, 20 May 1998)

Fig. 12.1B: Qasr al-Mshatta: detail of the great halls at the north end (APA02.2/SL21.5, 30 September 2002)

Qasr al-Mshatta

> *Suddenly drawing rein in front of Mashita, after a headlong dash at a herd of gazelle across the hadj road, we were astonished at the unexpected magnificence of the ruins, unknown to history, and unnamed in the maps. It has evidently been a palace of some ancient prince. … It must have stood out on the waste in solitary grandeur, a marvelous example of the sumptuousness and selfishness of ancient princes.* (Canon H. B. Tristram, *The Land of Moab*, 1873: 212)

Many passengers arriving at Amman's Queen Alia International Airport will be delighted by their introduction to Jordan. Visible just beyond the northern perimeter lie the massive ruins of a great square structure. This is Qasr al-Mshatta — the 'Winter Palace' — the greatest of the Umayyad 'Desert Palaces' **(Fig. 12.1A)**.

Palace is a legitimate term in this case, because of the scale and magnificence of the structure. It is 144 m square, it walls still stand up to 5 m high in places, and its internal buildings and surviving decoration are a significant draw for tourists. It was, moreover, a royal building, the work of the Umayyad caliph Walid II and dated to AD 743.

Qasr al-Mshatta is situated on the edge of the steppe, about 6 km northeast of the railway station and reservoir at Ziza (Jiza) (Fig. 14.1B). Caliph Walid II is remembered as a prince addicted to hunting and the desert; Tristram's encounters with herds of gazelle in the vicinity in 1872 reveal the continued abundance of game. Even now, with access roads and a major airport nearby, the place remains solitary on the plain, though the latter is now extensively cultivated.

Although it is massive and was extensively decorated, it seems never to have been completed. As the view shows, it was designed as a great square. The sole entrance is on the south side, with a hexagonal tower on either side. There are then four semi-circular towers and finally a circular one on each corner. The east and west sides have five successive semi-circular towers and there are another five along the rear wall. The towers are still massive and impressive from the air, or on the ground.

The interior was divided into three rectangular north–south areas, but only the central one was developed extensively. It is thought that the outer zones were for storage, and stabling camels and horses respectively. In the central area the foundations of buildings are visible, just to the left of the entrance, and the large rectangle on the right is the foundation of a mosque. Dominating this central zone, however, is the residence or great hall **(Fig. 12.1B).** Visible in the photograph are the dark interiors of the great barrel vaulted chambers, which flank a central trefoil planned hall. An indication of its status is that it was constructed of baked brick and not just sun-dried bricks (cf. Fig. 12.5B). The vaults are inspired by parallel work in Sassanian Mesopotamia.

The exterior of the encircling wall was elaborately decorated with relief sculpture — a mixture of floral and animal designs, and a variety of styles, drawing on both Hellenistic and Sassanian influences, especially in the form of the poses of the animals. Other motifs included carvings of trees, cornucopiae, vines, palmettes, animal and bird forms, comparable to those on the Dome of the Rock. This façade was presented to Emperor William II of Germany by the Sultan Abdulhamid and taken to Berlin (now in the Pergamon Museum) just before World War I. Fragments have survived at ground level, just beside the gate; these still give a hint of its intended magnificence.

Fig. 12.1A: Qasr al-Mshatta: panoramic view looking north (APA98/SL11.11, 13 May 1998)

Fig. 12.2B: Qasr Mushash: detail of the qasr and external cisterns (APA02.1/ SL1.27, 1 April 2002)

Qasr Mushash

Travelling on from Mshatta around the so-called 'Desert Castles', one might next stop at Muwaqqar 12 km to the northeast, but sadly only the large reservoir survives of the former Umayyad mansion. Next, however, is Qasr Mushash, 40 km east-southeast of Amman, a far more imposing but different set of ruins. In a very different environment, the *qasr* is much smaller and very simple, and the remains are far more varied and scattered. Although there is a significant trace (10%) of Late Roman (4th to 7th centuries AD) pottery, the evidence is overwhelmingly Umayyad — largely early 8th century.

Despite the arid environment **(Fig. 12.2A)** the place was plainly important; 18 distinct ruins are scattered over some 4 sq km on the north side of the Wadi Mushash. Prominent are hydraulic structures — dams, channels, at least three stone-lined reservoirs, several cisterns and *qanats* (cf. Fig. 11.8). This significant water supply was excessive for the accommodation. However, there are hints of cultivation and it is likely that passing travellers and flocks were catered for, thereby increasing the population. Seasonally we might envisage the black tents of nomads with their herds and flocks; at other times it might be passing traders, or government couriers, moving between the great centres of the early Islamic world, across this desert area to the broad trough of the Wadi Sirhan and down to the oasis of Al-Jauf in Arabia.

In the foreground of **Figure 12.2A** is a long rectangular reservoir, *c.* 18 x 7 m and more than 3 m deep — a large square one (*c.* 25 x 25 x 4.5 m) is out of sight beneath the helicopter — and beyond are the excavated rooms of a bath-suite, *c.* 15 x 10 m, in which were found a furnace, clay flue pipes set in the walls and pieces of marble from a floor supported on brick piers. Immediately east of the bath, earthworks outline a buried square courtyard structure *c.* 34.5 x 33 m. Together with the bath-suite this complex is reminiscent of the contemporary site at Qasr Ain es-Sil (Fig. 12.10B).

Various walls can be seen cutting across and alongside the wadi, probably to channel floodwater into cisterns. The most impressive of the latter is the circular one, 4.80 m in diameter (top of Fig. 12.2B), from which a channel (not visible) runs over 300 m to the east, to an even larger one.

Finally, the *'qasr'*, lies on a bend of the wadi in the distance, **(Fig. 12.2B)**. It is stone-built, *c.* 26 m square, with 13 rooms around a courtyard, adequate for *c.* 40 people. As can be seen in the left corner where there has been digging, the walls still survive to over a metre in height.

Mushash is probably a small Late Roman site subsequently developed in the Umayyad period to create a desert residence with conspicuous traces of luxury. The *qasr* may have functioned as a secure halting place for travellers, but most of the stored water would have been used to water plants and animals. The implied security seems to have been short-lived and the site may have declined sharply in the later 8th century, after the fall of the Umayyad dynasty.

Fig. 12.2A: Qasr Mushash: panoramic view looking east over part of the site on the Wadi Mushash (APA97/SL1.25, 27 May 1997)

Fig. 12.3B: Qasr al-Kharaneh: looking northwest (APA02.1/ SL2.19, 1 April 2002)

Qasr el-Kharaneh

Twenty years ago a visit to this extraordinary site, 55 km east of Amman, involved several kilometres on desert tracks marked only by cairns: with sharp stones beneath the tyres it was probably best only attempted with 4-wheel drive. The place itself was strikingly isolated in a way even now one can still sense, despite the highway nearby, helicopter pad, tourist buses and electricity pylons **(Fig. 12.3A).** In fact, it has not been quite so totally remote as appearances suggest, either in the distant past, or in much more recent times. Not far from the *qasr* is the large Epipalaeolithic site of Kharaneh IV, while in the 1920s and 30s the plateau here was a staging point on the airmail route from Egypt to the Persian Gulf and for the RAF.

The *qasr* was once believed to belong to the brief Persian occupation of Jordan in the early 7th century, but recent detailed research has argued convincingly for an Umayyad date. A score of painted early Arabic (Kufic) graffiti have been found on the inside walls, one of which has the date AD 710.

The place is startling in its solidity. It is *c.* 25 m square and still stands several metres high. The walls are made of courses of small stones, but it was originally entirely plastered over. At each corner is a slender and rather feeble-looking circular tower and three of the sides have similar semi-circular ones in the centre. The middle of the south wall has the sole doorway (to the right of which is a stone with Greek letters built into the foundation). 'Arrow slits' may have been for light, rather than defence. As the second photograph shows **(Fig. 12.3B)**, the interior comprises a small square courtyard, entirely surrounded by rooms on two storeys. All told there are 61 rooms: as the roofless section reveals, these had barrel-vaulted ceilings. Most of the rooms on the upper floor were probably accommodation; those on the ground floor, on either side of the entrance, were stables and the rest probably storerooms.

The purpose of the castle is now plausibly seen as a factor in the relationship between the Umayyad dynasty and the nomads of the deserts. Here, seasonally, tribes concentrated and could meet and negotiate their relationship with their rulers. Perhaps, as is happening today, there was some effort at creating a garden at the site, but early air photographs of 1918 and the 1920s show no traces of such work.

Fig. 12.3A: Qasr al-Kharaneh: panoramic view looking southwest (APA02.1/ SL2.4, 1 April 2002)

Fig. 12.4B: Qusayr Amra: looking south (APA02.1/SL2.34, 1 April 2002)

Qusayr Amra

Although only 13 km northeast of Qasr al-Kharaneh, the landscape here is more attractive and water from the Wadi Butm provided at least seasonal vegetation. Here, too, a recent highway has made this once remote site easily accessible **(Fig. 12.4A).**

Once again the date is Umayyad and, as at Kharaneh (Fig. 12.3), it is thought that occupation was seasonal. Instead of a massive castle, however, the owner created a delightful complex consisting of an audience chamber and bath suite. In **Figure 12.4B** we are looking at the doorway into the Audience Chamber. The tall chamber is roofed by a triple barrel-vault, although there are lower vaults to the rear covering other areas. To the left is the integrated bath building with both barrel vaults and a dome. The interior is superb. Every surface is plastered and almost everything has been decorated. Human figures abound and show the richness and colour of the Umayyad period. One group of figures depicts the Umayyad Caliph Walid I (AD 705–715) together with those other masters of his world, the Byzantine Emperor at Constantinople, Visigothic King of Spain, Shah of Persia, Negus of Abyssinia and — less certainly — rulers of India and China. All around are scenes of hunting, athletics, craftsmanship and several notable scantily clothed women. This remarkable building and astonishing art, reflects not just its Romano-Syrian roots, but also the shifts of the Umayyad culture. Because of this it has been adopted as a World Heritage Site.

Outside is a small, enclosed courtyard, with a deep well tapping into the groundwater of the nearby wadi. The depth and the quantities needed, explain the elaborate wheel-house with lifting mechanism. Also needed in abundance, from time to time, would have been fuel to heat the water and warm the underfloor areas in the bath.

Fig. 12.4A: Qusayr Amra: panorama looking west (APA97/SL1.36, 27 May 1997)

Fig. 12.5B: Qasr al-Tuba: looking south (APA98/SL14.23, 14 May 1998)

The Jilat Dam and Qasr al-Tuba

The final 'Desert Castle' to be illustrated lies further out into the desert, 50 km to the southeast of Qasr al-Kharaneh. First, however, the traveller encounters at the halfway point, one of those unexpected but common traces of human activity in the desert.

The Wadi Jilat is a tributary of the Wadi Dhobai. At one point the wadi has cut a deeper than expected channel in the barren desert of this region and it was here that a dam was built across the seasonal stream. As the photograph shows **(Fig. 12.5A)**, the dam is well preserved and, after recent clearance of silt upstream, is again creating a small lake. The wall is 58 m long, 5–5.5 m wide and about 6 m high. It is vertical on the upstream side; on the downstream side it is stepped slightly and further strengthened on that side by three buttresses. There are important prehistoric sites nearby and traces of a more recent beduin mosque. Dating is uncertain. Nabataean, Roman and Umayyad have all been suggested. The recent discovery of Nabataean sherds in the mortar of the wall reinforce the possibility of an early date. Architecturally it accords with Roman parallels. It may well be Nabataean but in use throughout the subsequent centuries.

Qasr al-Tuba is the most remote and largest of the Umayyad period desert residences **(Fig. 12.5B).** It is *c.* 145 x 70 m and dated to AD 743–4. It was intended to be immense but was in fact never completed. The two halves were probably intended to be symmetrical but, as the photograph shows, only part was completed. Barrel vaulted chambers, with courses of baked brick surmounted by mud-brick — a novelty in these structures, were constructed in one half. Most of the site, including all of the southern half, appears only as the foundation levels visible in the photograph.

Fig. 12.5A: Wadi Jilat Dam: looking west (APA98/ SL14.10, 14 May 1998)

Fig. 12.6B: Qastal: looking west (APA98/SL11.20, 13 May 1998)

Al-Qastal

The site is centred on a small rise overlooking a wadi to the north and fertile soils all around. It lies 22 km south of Amman, just west of the Desert Highway, a short distance before the airport turnoff. Jiza (Fig. 14.1B) is 5 km further south and Qasr el-Mshatta (Fig. 12.1) 6 km to the east.

Qastal is a large site. There are several prominent buildings around the *qasr*, but others have been found in a wider circle and the original settlement seems to have been a kilometre to the southwest at Zabayir al-Qastal. Qastal itself may have had settlement as early as the 6th century and there was certainly occupation through until at least Abassid times.

Early visitors thought the *qasr* was Roman and identified components with suitable names — *'praetorium', 'principia'.* We now know it is Umayyad and recent research has begun to restore some of what was so striking to visitors in the 19th century. Tristram in 1872, described the ruins at length and drew a well-preserved stretch of wall and tower; Gray Hill a few years later wrote of descending 40 feet into a multi-chambered cistern and Brünnow and von Domaszewski, a generation later still, illustrated their great book with photographs of tall walls and impressive ruins. More recently, development of the modern village began to obscure the remains. The *qasr* itself became a dump then, scandalously, this important early Islamic building was partly deliberately destroyed to make way for a mansion. The views here show how the site has again begun to blossom through clearance, survey, excavation and a programme to enlist the interest of the villagers.

The panoramic view **(Fig. 12.6A)** looks out over the fertile plain with the core of Qastal in the foreground centre. Several other components of the site, mainly hydraulic, are visible on the ground: the North Reservoir beside the airport road; a dam sweeping for several hundred metres across the wadi to the northwest and another to the east; and the West Reservoir a few hundred metres west of the road. As for cisterns, a recent survey has recorded nearly 100. Just west of the West Reservoir is where the newly discovered building — a second bath(?) — was uncovered with its superb early Islamic mosaic floors.

In the detailed view **(Fig. 12.6B)** we are looking down over the *qasr*, mosque (right) and early cemetery (above the *qasr*). The latter includes several early Arabic inscriptions and the mosque is one of the earliest to have a minaret as an integral element of the initial design. The *qasr* is square, *c.* 68 x 69 m. It has large circular towers on each corner, with three semi-circular ones on all sides, except the east where the main entrance lies. The interior is a large courtyard overlying the massive multi-chambered cistern described by Gray Hill. Surrounding it are rooms which once stood two storeys high and included both extensive mosaic flooring and ornately carved stonework.

Fig. 12.6A: Qastal: looking north (APA02.2/ SL21.20, 30 September 2002)

Fig. 12.7A: Umm el-Walid: panoramic view looking west over the ancient and modern settlement (APA98/ SL11.36, 13 May 1998)

Umm el-Walid

The ruins of this ancient town lie *c.* 30km south of Amman, at a junction of ancient roads in the zone between the *Via Nova Traiana, c.* 12 km to the west, and sections of a desert road, *c.* 8 km to the east. It is a large site (*c.* 4 ha) and has begun to attract very useful fieldwork and analysis in recent years. The site includes, to the northwest, a cemetery with monumental tomb and Greek epitaph and there is good evidence from pottery for a Nabataean and Roman phase. The 'town wall', reported by an early visitor, might also be a survivor of a large Roman period settlement. Most of what is easily visible today, however, is apparently Umayyad.

Figure 12.7A provides a panorama covering the entire settlement. On the lower left edge is the West Qasr (*c.* 46 m square). Even through the collapse of walls, one can see the outline of a square structure without projecting towers, a central courtyard and rooms built against the interior of the walls. It is probably Umayyad, but may overlie, or be the rebuilding of, a Late Roman caravanserai. To the right of this structure is a large area with traces of buried and ruined buildings, many of which include Roman pottery.

In the bottom right quadrant (the northeast) are several important structures. Most notable is the sharp outline of a cleared structure, the East Qasr. Just above it (to the west), however, partly obscured by recent houses, is the smaller Central Qasr (48 m square) and beyond that again, also obscured now, are two ancient temples. In the bottom right corner is the outline of a small rare Umayyad mosque.

The East Qasr **(Rear Cover)** is almost exactly 71 m square, but has small circular towers at each corner and three semi-circular ones on the sides, except the east where there is an entrance in the centre. Thirty-one rooms, each with its own entrance, surround the central courtyard. Sizes vary, but there are repetitions in the pattern and many are square. Each had an arch supporting a flat roof that ran around the entire circuit. The building material includes a great deal salvaged from old structures. The overall design is very similar to the slightly smaller Khan es-Zabib *c.* 25 km to the southeast.

Especially interesting for this place is the recent work done on some structures first reported a century ago. **Figure 12.7B** depicts the western of two successive dams across the wadi, 2 km to the east. It is 187 m long and made of masonry reminiscent of that at the East Qasr. The intention was to create a lake and divert water onto an area of fields farmed intensively nearby. The building visible at the south end includes a wine press and was fed from a channel (in the background) bringing water from the other dam upstream (top, just round the curve of the wadi).

Fig. 12.7B: Umm el-Walid: the west dam on the Wadi al-Qanatir east of the East Qasr (APA02.2/ SL28.32, 30 September 2002)

Fig. 12.8B: Aqaba: looking southeast (APA98/SL42.11, 21 May 1998)

Aqaba

A succession of sites at the head of the Gulf of Aqaba reveal settlement from the Chalcolithic onwards. The significance of the place lies in its location: a port giving access to the Red Sea ports and out into the ocean beyond for the trade with and through India; northwest across the Negev Desert to the Mediterranean; at the start of the great route north up the Wadi Araba to the Dead Sea and Palestine; northeast through the Wadi Yitm to Edom, Moab and Syria; and southeast into the Hejaz and South Arabia. Not just as an import centre either, but also the port through which the copper of the mines in the Wadi Araba could be exported (cf. Fig. 11.10).

The fullest flowering seems to have begun in the Nabataean period; later it was not just a Roman town, but the southern terminus of the great *Via Nova Traiana* (cf. Fig. 9.10B), which had started out in southern Syria far to the north. In the early Christian Roman period Aila — as it was called — was the base of a legion and later the seat of a bishop. The latter is mentioned in AD 630, negotiating with the forces of Islam, and the place soon benefited from being part of the new empire.

Excavations on the Islamic city of Ayla, of the mid-7th to 12th centuries, recovered the plan of a rectangular city whose plan is astonishingly like a small version (only 165 x 140 m, 2.3 ha) of the Roman legionary fortress at Lejjun (cf. Fig. 10.5). There was of course another Late Roman legion at Aila itself and the suspicion is that its fortress was similar to Lejjun and its ruins inspired the plan of the Islamic town.

Most of this Islamic town is clear in **Figure 12.8A.** One wall has been lost beneath the Corniche Road across the centre, a corner destroyed on the bottom right and a shallow wadi runs diagonally across the site. The rectangular outline, the succession of U-shaped towers along the walls and the gates in the middle of each side, are all visible. Internally the notable features are a street running from the Egyptian Gate (whose twin towers are on the right in **Fig. 12.8B**) across to the Hejaz Gate opposite. At its mid-point is a pavilion. To the left is the outline of the largest building excavated, a rectangular enclosure with internal colonnades, an Abbasid rebuilding of an earlier Umayyad mosque.

Fig. 12.8A: Aqaba: panorama looking north across the modern marina, the Islamic town, Corniche Road and part of the modern city (APA98/ SL42.17, 21 May 1998)

Fig. 12.9A: El-Fedein (APA98/ SL3.26 (RHB), 9 May 1998)

El-Fedein

Amongst the houses of modern Mafraq and just west of the railway station is the succession of ruins which comprise what was the original settlement at this location. El-Fedein is mentioned in early Islamic writers, but recent work has shown that other periods are extensively represented. The *Via Nova Traiana* passed a few kilometres east of Mafraq, but a spur seems to have run towards El-Fedein and probably on to Jarash. In this photograph **(Fig. 12.9A)** are the remains of a large rectangular fortress; in the bottom right corner of this is a Late Roman church. In the centre is a Late Roman and Umayyad house, which once boasted important mosaics. At the bottom is a small square building, which may have been an early Islamic bath suite. Not so easily seen is the Bronze Age tell at the bottom right, in the corner between the dirt road and the asphalt one.

Fig. 12.9B: Khirbat al-Makhul: looking east across the Middle and Late Islamic hilltop residence (APA98/ SL10.24, 13 May 1998)

Khirbat al-Makhul

Khirbat al-Makhul is a very unusual site, located on the peak of a conical hill *c.* 6 km north of Zarqa **(Fig. 12.9B).** From the summit (*c.* 660 m) there is a superb view in all directions, including over the valleys of the Wadis az-Zarqa and ad-Dulayl.

The site consists of concentric ranges of rooms, arranged in an oval pattern around the summit. The entrance seems to have been at the northeast side. Rooms are generally rectilinear and there are traces of arches for vaulted roofs. In the centre is a large L-shaped building with a cistern; part of it was probably a mosque.

Despite the poor quality of much of the construction and the unexpected overall design, the result is solid. The large number of rooms may point to the place being used as a caravanserai.

Some of the pottery recorded on the surface may be pre-Islamic. Most, however, is Islamic in date with the particular concentration of activity from the later Early Islamic period onwards.

Fig. 12.10B: Azraq Oasis — Qasr Ain es-Sil: the Early Islamic residence and farm (APA98/ SL 33.12, 18 May 1998)

Azraq Oasis: Pools and Mansion

After Palmyra, the oasis at Al-Azraq ('The Blue') is the largest in the Syrian Desert and consists of northern pools at Azraq Duruz and southern at Azraq Shishan. Though once extensive they have been entirely pumped dry in very recent years. Inevitably the pools attracted human activity from an early time. There is a large Roman fort at Duruz, later remodelled extensively in the Middle Ages (Fig. 13.5), small Roman forts on the fringes of the Azraq Basin (cf. Fig. 10.8) and the two Early Islamic structures illustrated here. (Today the northern pools are gone, and the small pool at Shishan has been artifically created by pumping water *back* to Azraq.)

On the western edge of the Azraq Shishan pools the silted irregular outline of a large reservoir can still be seen, its massive walls strengthened by semicircular and triangular buttresses **(Fig. 12.10A)**. In the bottom left corner, a circular structure, linked to the reservoir, has been exposed by excavation. Hidden under the silt and among the marshland reeds are two other walls, which run out from the northwestern and southwestern corners of the reservoir and extend in great loops around the north and south of the marsh. They seem to have been intended to enclose the whole marsh in a circuit of about 2.5–4 km, but were not completed. In 1998 there was still water in much of the reservoir and in the adjacent marsh; in this image the pools are dry and the marsh showing the signs of a recent fire.

Dredging of the reservoir in the 1980's, brought out numerous stone blocks carved in relief, with stylized figures of birds and animals. Although the site was doubtless of importance in the Roman period, the principal features most closely parallel the irrigated gardens of early Islamic 'desert castles' like that at Qasr al-Hayr al-Gharbi northeast of Palmyra.

Figure 12.10B shows the Umayyad residence and farmstead at Qasr Ain es-Sil. It lies beside a spring on the northern edge of the Azraq Oasis, 1.75 km northeast of the Castle (Fig. 13.5). The core of the site is a small crude square (17.7 x 17.6 m) structure. After a vestibule there is a small courtyard with 8 rooms opening off. There is a staircase to the roof. Two adjacent rooms contained olive presses and a room adjoining the northeast has two bread ovens (*taboun*). Along the west side (left) a bath suite consisting of two hot rooms with floors raised on brick pillars, a cold room and a changing room, some with red-painted plaster walls, was added.

On both east and north sides (right), the photograph shows foundations of several other structures. Some abut the *qasr*, many are very regular in their layout and in total they cover about four times the area of the main structure. Curving round the top of the *qasr* is a long wall, *c.* 1 m wide, curving out west from the site, then south, with various openings and spurs, for over 2.5 km. It seems to have been used for water, or soil control, or as a land boundary, and adds to the picture of the site as a farm cropping olives as is again the case today.

Pottery and other artefacts are overwhelmingly Umayyad; perhaps an early farmstead given a luxury element, then extensively developed as land was enclosed and irrigated. A curiosity is the basalt central column of one olive-press — part of a milestone of AD 208/10, evidently scavenged from the Roman road just to the west.

Fig. 12.10A: Azraq Oasis — Azraq Shishan: Umayyad reservoir, looking southwest (APA02/ SL4.3, 1 April 2002)

Fig. 13.1B: Kerak: looking west over the castle (APA98/ SL36.29, 20 May 1998)

Kerak

Kerak lies at a strategically important point in the midst of the rich agricultural lands on the plateau between the Wadi Mujib and Wadi el-Hasa in central Jordan. Its forerunners, the southern Moabite capital of Kir-Hareset and the subsequent Nabataean town of Characmoab stood at the intersection of major routes. The King's Highway is crossed by a lateral route coming up the Wadi Kerak from the Dead Sea and continuing east to the desert at Qatrana (site of a Hajj fort, Ch. 14). Under Roman rule it developed further, as one of the major cities of the province of Arabia, even striking its own coinage in the early 3rd century. Although there is no explicit evidence, it was surely an important garrison place in Late Roman Jordan. In the Middle Ages it came to be dominated by the great castle, which largely obliterated the ruins of earlier periods.

As **Figure 13.1A** shows, the town and castle occupy a steep-sided plateau, surrounded by deeply incised wadis, which provide natural defences. The scale is deceptive — note the size of vehicles on the road running along the northern limit of the town (foreground). The castle at the far end of the town (the south) sits on a ridge, which commands the town and the intersection of routes. In this view we are looking due south, along the alignment of the Kings Highway/ *Via Nova Traiana,* with the Dead Sea off to the right almost 20 km to the west and nearly 1.5 km lower.

The origins of the castle lie in the mid-12th century. Expanding eastwards from Jerusalem, for economic reasons as much as anything else, the Crusader kings of Jerusalem started granting land to individuals. Pagan the Butler was granted permission by King Fulk at Jerusalem to improve the defences in 'Oultrejourdain'. One result was the great castle at Kerak, built in 1142 on the site of the ancient city. The castle continued to be strengthened by Pagan's successors (especially the notorious Reynald de Châtillon, 1177–1187), because of repeated attacks by Nur al-Din and Salah ad-Din (Saladin) between 1170 and 1187. Reynald broke a treaty safeguarding the passage of caravans through the area, and used the castle as a base for raiding. Salah ad-Din eventually took the castle in November 1188.

Figure 13.1B shows the massive and near-impregnable defences (note the buses on the road immediately below the east glacis). The castle lies on an artificial island of the plateau, *c.* 200 m long and varying between 110 and 140 m wide. Its constructional history has yet to be fully investigated, but there seem to have been two distinct Crusader phases followed by modifications to the defences and internal changes and additions in the Mamluk period. The Crusader church (just above the tall tower in the centre foreground) was altered to a mosque and a Mamluk palace was built at the south end (left in the photograph). In this period the castle and town were the centre of an administrative district extending from Ziza to Aqaba. In the 13th and 14th centuries it was used as a school (and place of exile for problem members of the royal families). Ottoman control came and went, but it was an important administrative centre of late Ottoman Jordan.

On the left in **Figure 13.1B**, one of the two parallel roads passes through the artificial ditch, dug to strengthen the southern defences. Above the ditch, running north is the walled enclosure of a great reservoir. The castle defences are lozenge-shaped. In the foreground is the steep masonry wall of the glacis. On the right is the massive wall of the north front and the North Ditch separating it from the town. A few traces of the vaulted corridors that honeycomb the interior are visible.

Fig. 13.1A: Kerak: looking south over the town and castle (APA98/ SL36.19, 20 May 1998)

Fig. 13.2B: Shaubak: looking west (APA98/ SL38.34, 20 May 1998)

Shaubak (Mont Real)

Unlike Kerak, the early history of Shaubak is slight — no more than a scatter of sherds implying occupation in Nabataean times. The Crusader castle was, therefore, apparently the first major structure on the site. Interestingly, however, 11 km to the east is the Roman (?) fortlet and caravanserai of Khirbat Qannas and 9 km further again, is the Roman fort of Da'ajaniya (Fig. 10.7) on the fringe of the desert.

The site is in the Jebel Shera range, 75 km south of Kerak and 25 north of Petra. As **Figure 13.2A** shows, the castle is strategically situated on the summit (1,412 m) of a cone-shaped hill, in a region of little settlement. The area was heavily wooded until the early 20th century when its trees were cut down for the Hejaz Railway. Its importance lay in its location on the King's Highway (the Roman *Via Nova Traiana*), which was a major Pilgrim Road in the Middle Ages (Ch. 14). This was also the inland route from Damascus to Egypt, by-passing the Crusader principalities along the Mediterranean.

Shaubak was built in 1115/6, as part of a screen of fortresses created by King Baldwin I of Jerusalem, to protect the eastern approaches to the new Crusader territories in the Levant. For a short period it was the administrative centre for what the Franks called Oultrejourdain and, even after it was superseded by Kerak in 1142, it continued to be an important element in this line of defence. The wider landscape was productive and Crusader sources write of the vicinity as one with 'fertile soil, which produces abundant supplies of grain, wine and oil' and contemporary sources record that the inhabitants included, knights, soldiers and peasants.

The Crusader phase was brief. Having captured Kerak in 1188, Salah ad-Din (Saladin) moved on to Shaubak in 1189 and both castles became part of the Ayyubids' family estate, with Saladin's brother ruling this territory. The Ayyubids added further fortifications, but the Mamluks seized the castle in 1250. Further damage was sustained in 1280 and 1293, but the Sultan Lajin rebuilt the castle at the end of the 13th century and much of what is visible may be his work.

Ottoman control was short-lived and the castle passed to local tribal rulers for almost three centuries. In 1840 the retreating troops of Ibrahim Pasha dynamited it; in the next half century Ottoman control was re-established. The castle, however, was left to villagers who lived in security within its shattered defences till the mid-20th century. Although one commentator a half century ago observed that it 'hardly repays a closer look', it has been extensively consolidated and is again an impressive fortress.

The castle is oval shaped (*c.* 175 x 90 m) with tall masonry walls marked with a series of semi-circular and rectangular towers. At three points massive, rectilinear projections included suites of rooms. As **Figure 13.2B** shows, the internal rooms, both in these bastions and in the courtyard area, are often two storeyed and barrel vaulted. It seems that many of the settlers lived inside the walls and the remains include two churches, one dated by an inscription to 1118.

Fig. 13.2A: Shaubak: looking southeast (APA98/ SL38.38, 20 May 1998)

Fig. 13.3A: Wu'eira (APA02.2/ SL25.30, 30 September 2002)

Wu'eira

Petra is best known for its Nabataean and Roman remains, but the Crusader period too is etched on this marvellous landscape. The region remained a prosperous one and Crusader sources note the string of villages through which travellers passed en route to Wadi Musa (itself described as 'rich in the fruits of the earth'). Like Shaubak, the castle in the fertile valley just outside Petra was the work of the Frankish king, Baldwin I of Jerusalem. According to ancient stories, he had been petitioned by Christian monks living in the monastery of Jebel Harun inside Petra, but it is more likely that the new fortress was simply part of the succession of castles he had built east of the Jordan.

Although a fort was built at al-Habees, a high point inside Petra, to permit signalling overland to Jerusalem, the main fortress was located in Wadi Musa, what the Crusaders called Li Vaux Moise (Wadi Mousa or the Valley of Moses). It was abandoned in 1189, the last of the eastern fortresses to surrender to Salah ad-Din after the Crusaders were defeated at the Battle of Hattin (AD 1187), and lost their territories east of the Jordan.

Today the castle is called Wu'eira. It lies in an area of nobbly, rocky hills overlooking a narrow road pass **(Fig. 13.3A).** The castle is rectilinear, *c.* 100 x 80 m. Along the walls are towers; there is a bailey inside and rooms against the walls all around. It is poorly preserved, and the mounds of tumbled masonry and rock-cut features are hard to make sense of at ground level. There are, however, at least two places where tall walls of towers survive (both in the bottom left quarter).

In **Figure 13.3B** the deep shadow in the narrow ravine guarding the eastern side is strongly emphasized. Access to the castle was over the outcrop east of the ravine, down a flight of rock-cut steps (top left) to a narrow path (left), which led the visitor to a bridge. The latter is the centre of the view and, as can be seen, the path, in part, cuts right through a rock before reaching the bridge.

Fig. 13.3B: Wu'eira (APA02.2/ SL25.31, 30 September 2002)

Fig. 13.4B: Qala'at er-Rabad: looking north (APA98/ SL23.13, 16 May 1998)

Qal'at er-Rabad

Jordan is well known for its great medieval castles, many the work of 12th century Frankish Crusaders. Qal'at er-Rabad, 16 km west of Jarash and just west of Ajlun, however, is the work of their Muslim opponents. A 13th century Arab writer reported that it was built in 1184–1185 by 'Azz al-Din Ausama, during the rule of the Ayyubid Salah al-Din (Saladin). However, according to an inscription, it was considerably extended 30 years later to strengthen the gateway and provide more cohesion to its components. What we see today may be essentially the work of this phase.

The castle was located on the heights overlooking the Jordan Valley, at a point where it could command the approach to the fertile plateau, thus thwarting further expansion of the Frankish kingdom, which had its own great castle of Belvoir on the far side of the River Jordan.

Today, the castle is still visible from miles around. Looking west **(Fig. 13.4A)** one sees the wide views open to the garrison and the commanding position of the castle on a steep-sided outcrop above a valley. Closer inspection **(Fig. 13.4B)** underscores the great bulk and strength of the castle itself, *c.* 70 m square, with massive square towers. Its squat appearance contrasts with Frankish examples at Kerak, Shaubak and Wu'eira (Figs 13.1–13.3). The tall walls of fine masonry tower above the landscape, and the partial collapse on one side allows a glimpse down into a tangled interior of courtyard, stairs, windows and exposed corridors. Even today, in the unthreatening modern landscape of villages and fields, the place carries an aura of power, and it is a notable example of Arab architecture of the time.

Fig. 13.4A: Qala'at er-Rabad: looking west (APA98/ SL23.9, 16 May 1998)

Fig. 13.5A: Azraq Castle: looking north (APA02.1/ SL4.12, 1 April 2002)

Azraq Duruz

The 'castle' beside the northern pools at the Azraq Oasis, is a familiar feature in the landscape. When the German, then British air forces, took air photographs in 1917 and in the 1920s, there was no settlement around it. The village appeared in the 1930s for the Druze refugees from Syria and in the past decade the development of a highway, from Aqaba through Azraq to Baghdad, has transformed the former village into a town. Fortunately, the castle is insulated and remains a striking landmark **(Fig. 13.5A).** Almost gone however, are the last traces of the northern pools, the remnants of which are just visible to the right of the castle; even a decade ago they stretched up to the highway.

As at the southern part of the oasis (Fig. 12.10A), it was water that gave the place its outstanding importance: perennial and abundant springs, great open pools, which transformed into shallow but extensive lakes in winter with a wide and abundant variety of wildlife in the marshes, as well as immense flocks of migratory birds annually.

The Romans fortified the place, and the 'castle' still bears the distinctive design of a Roman fort **(Fig. 13.5B).** Milestones show Roman interest going back to AD 208/10, but the fort itself is dated broadly by Latin inscriptions to the late 3rd/ early 4th century AD. Azraq lay on a major trade route from central Arabia and the Gulf beyond. More than that, however, it lay on a transhumance route for the nomads of the desert. Controlling this immense water supply controlled the people who depended on it for themselves, and their flocks and herds. The Roman entrance was almost certainly in the middle of the east side (behind the palms on the left). The fort is a near square, 79 x 72 m (0.57 ha), with rectangular towers projecting *c.* 1 m at each corner. Rooms were built against the wall all around, with many given over for stables. Staircases gave access to an upper storey. On the west wall (right) is the HQ of the garrison (left in the figure).

There was evidently significant modification in the Middle Ages. The present gate enters through a tower (the white-topped structure in the middle of the furthest wall) on the face of which is a mediaeval machicolation and below that an Arabic inscription recording construction of the 'castle' in AD 1237:

Bismillah. The construction of this blessed castle was ordered by the seeker after God, 'Izz ad-Din Aubak, majordomo of al-Malik al-Mu'azzam, under the direction of 'Ali son of Al-Hajib and 'Ali son of Qarjala, in the year 634.

In the middle of the courtyard is a small mosque. Taken together with the evidence from the southern pools (cf. Fig. 12.10A), it seems clear the oasis remained important in Islamic times and was indeed heavily refortified in the 13th century.

Fig. 13.5B: Azraq Castle: looking south (APA02.1/ SL4.20, 1 April 2002)

Fig. 13.6B: Jabal Harun: looking south (APA03/ SL26.20 (RHB), 30 September 2003)

Jabal Harun

High on a hill, 1,350 m above sea level and with panoramic views in all directions, about one kilometre west-southwest of central Petra, is a striking white-building **(Fig. 13.6A).** This is the hill of Jabal Harun and the building is a 14th century Islamic shrine *(weli).*

'Harun' is Aaron, brother of Moses, a major religious figure for Jews, Christians and Muslims. Here, reputedly, are deposited the remains of this holy man in a shrine of great antiquity. The medieval Islamic building is dated by an Arabic inscription to AD 1338–9, the Mamluk period, but it overlies a much older structure. In part this earlier structure is an ancient (Nabataean? or Roman?) rock-cut tomb with multiple chambers. However, the Muslim shrine incorporates pieces of church marble and it has been argued that it was built on part of what was, by then, a larger, but ruined Christian church. Certainly the shrine was popular in late Roman and Early Islamic times (below) and there were still two 'Melkite' Christian monks resident there in AD 1217, in the last reference we have from the Crusader period. When Sultan Baibars was there in 1267 it was deserted. Burckhardt used a planned pilgrimage to this shrine as his pretext in 1812 for the first known western visit to Petra itself in modern times. It seems, however, that the shrine itself was not actually visited until Irby and Mangles were there in 1818.

The detailed view **(Fig. 13.6B)** shows the shrine on its peak, but also the large structure on the wide terrace below the summit. As the photograph shows, the building is under excavation (by a Finnish team whose camp is behind in the lee of an outcrop). The building itself has long been identified as a monastery, and excavation has now given dates of 5th to at least 8th century AD — i.e. Late Roman to Abassid times. Evidently it was both a monastery and a hostel for pilgrims. Overall it is *c.* 62 x 48 m and consisted of a large church with courtyards surrounded by rooms off to either side.

Fig. 13.6A: Jabal Harun: looking east (APA00/ SL6.27 (RHB), 14 September 2000)

Fig. 13.7B: Aqaba Castle: looking southeast (APA98/ SL42.4, 20 May 1998)

Aqaba Castle

The Umayyad town of Ayla (cf. Fig. 12.8) was occupied down to the 12th century. Then, in 1116, the Crusader King of Jerusalem made a raid on the place, which seems to have brought settlement to an end. The Crusaders were there until 1170, but no castle has been located. The castle on the island in the Gulf — Jazirat Fara'un (Ile de Graye) — is now known to be Ayyubid and the best guess is that the Crusader castle underlies the later Arab castle illustrated here.

The castle (on the shore at the eastern end of the bay at modern Aqaba) is well preserved and has recently been consolidated **(Fig. 13.7A).** Recently excavated 9th–11th century pottery, implies that in origin it may have been Ayyubid, or had an Ayyubid predecessor. As it stands, however, it is Mamluk; indeed, an inscription of Sultan Qansawh al-Ghawri (1501–1516) records its building:

> *... blessed and auspicious fort our lord the ruling Sultan al-Malik al-Ashraf abu al-Nasr Qansawh al-Ghawri, Sultan of Islam and the Muslims, slayer [of the unbelievers and the polytheists], reviver of justice in the universe ... the Sultan al-Malik al-Ashraf abu al-Nasr Qansawh al-Ghawri, may God glorify his victories through Muhammad and his house! This blessed fort was the work of the Amir Khayir Bey al-'Ala'i the builder dated [in the year 920 AH] (= AD1514/5)* (trans. H. Glidden)

A contemporary Arab historian reports this sultan as building 'a khan with towers flanking its gate and installed in its repositories for the goods of the pilgrims'. In other words it was both a castle and a pilgrim safe house.

It was still occupied in Late Ottoman times through to the Arab Revolt during the First World War. The raised Corniche Road in front of it may overlie a high bank, which was still visible in 1917 and was apparently intended to deflect water from the adjacent wadi away from the castle and village that grew up around it.

As **Figure 13.7B** shows, the castle is square (56 x 56 m) with large circular towers projecting at each corner one has been destroyed. The gate is massive, with projecting towers protecting the approach to a narrow doorway. Inside, an extensive courtyard is surrounded by rooms for accommodation, stabling and stores.

Fig. 13.7A: Aqaba Castle: looking south over the Corniche Road and castle to the Gulf of Aqaba (APA98/ SL41.37, 20 May 1998)

Fig. 13.8B: Majdalein (APA98/ SL35.34, 20 May 1998)

Majdalein

It is easy to understand the attraction of the locality: the wadi below the settlement could be tapped for water, while the population farmed the rich arable lands stretching off beyond **(Fig. 13.8A).** The extent of the site is unclear — ground survey measured *c.* 400 x 200 m, but noted traces in the fields beyond. The latter shows well from the air — indeed, in the panoramic view one can see marks of apparent enclosures in the wheat field and again in the ploughed field on either side of the road junction. Sadly, farming is likely to destroy both parts very soon.

Nineteenth century travellers were impressed by these extensive ruins: in 1851 de Saulcy wrote of the 'vast ruins of a city' and others described ruins and buried traces everywhere. There has been no excavation, but surface sherding gives a fairly clear picture; Iron Age, Nabataean and Roman are all present, but overwhelmingly the pottery is medieval. As so often, we see a site continually, if not continuously, occupied from early times onwards. What is unusual here is that after an apparent break of several centuries, the place was rebuilt, over the Late Roman ruins, as a large village of the 12th century and later.

Visitors report buildings, often apparently of more than one storey, and some at least later reconstruction on much older foundations. As the detailed view **(Fig. 13.8B)** shows, most are square or rectangular. They extend in a curve around the rim of the wadi. There is no planning involved, but the layout is orderly, with buildings often at least generally aligned on one another. Also visible, just left of the road junction, is a rectangular reservoir.

Fig. 13.8A: Majdalein (APA98/ SL35.33, 20 May 1998)

14. THE OTTOMAN AND BRITISH EMPIRES

JORDAN has been part of someone's empire throughout most of its recorded history — and that continued until the middle of the 20th century. Although imperial powers are usually great builders and often think on a grand scale, neither the Ottoman nor British Empires are well represented in the Jordanian landscape. The former was in decline throughout much of its history and relatively uninterested in a distant, thinly populated province. The British Empire in Jordan lasted only a generation. But there are important traces and their relative novelty makes their preservation that much more important.

Within the ancient Islamic world there were seven great pilgrim routes leading to Mecca. One of these — the Darb al-Hajj al-Shami, the Syrian Pilgrimage Road — ran from Damascus, through the length of Jordan, to reach the Arabian peninsula. The actual route taken was variable. The key factor was security. Thus, until the 16th century the Pilgrim Road ran mainly along the line of the King's Highway in the west of Jordan, where it passed through relatively settled landscapes punctuated by ancient strongpoints such as Kerak. However, the desert route was flatter and shorter, and when security could be assured pilgrims followed that line and provision was made for their needs. Security was achieved in the early Ottoman period and a desert route developed which remained in use through until the 20th century. Today, one of the principal traces of Ottoman rule are the forts of the Hajj Road, along the edge of the steppe, which the Ottoman sultans provided (Figs 14.1–14.3). Selim I (1512–1520) and Suleiman the Magnificent (1520–1566) are prominent in this effort, but the system as a whole was a patchwork of new work and refurbished older buildings, all of it spread over several centuries. Ten of the forts lie in Jordan. The best preserved are those close to the modern Desert Highway. After Ma'an the route branches off to the southeast, into Saudi Arabia, but the fort at Aqaba remained in use for pilgrims from Egypt. The principal function of the forts was to provide security and to control water points. As their positioning was determined by the availability of water (Fig. 14.1B), they are spaced irregularly and sometimes two or three days travel apart. One example from each of the two main phases of building — the 16th century (Fig. 14.2) and 18th century (Fig. 14.3) — are illustrated, as well as stretches of the 'road' itself (Fig. 14.1A).

One area in which the Ottoman period is relatively well represented is in the highlands of the northwest. The rich soils, good rainfall pattern and attractive little valleys supported settlement and some of this is beginning to be recognized. One type of structure which survives is the water mill, which took advantage of the small perennial streams around Jarash in particular (Fig. 14.4).

In recent years there has been a growing recognition of the significance of the late Ottoman period in Jordan and interest in exploring and preserving surviving examples of 19th century buildings, villages and khans. Most have been overlain by rapid modern development or destroyed entirely, but a few are on view in some of the older centres of 19th century Jordan such as Kerak, Salt and Irbid (Figs 13.1; 14.5B; 14.10B), as well as the stations on the Hejaz Railway (Fig. 14.6) (most notably King Abdullah's Palace in Ma'an).

Perhaps the single most important legacy of the late Ottoman period to Jordan was the introduction of two modern forms of transport; the Hejaz Railway (Fig. 14.6) and, right at the end of Ottoman rule, the aeroplane and its airfields (Fig. 14.8). And, of course, the beginnings of aerial photography: Ch. 4.

Several battles of the First World War were fought in Jordan and traces remain of extensive trenches (Fig. 14.7A). Most of the police forts of the British period are still intact. Unlike those of the Ottoman period they are found not just along the edge of the steppe, but often far out into the desert. In this respect they parallel the Roman period and some examples lie close to Roman forts (Fig. 14.7B).

The airfields, first laid out by Turks and Germans operating in Palestine and Transjordan in World War I, were soon taken over by the British, who established the Royal Air Force at Marka (Amman) and at other bases in Transjordan, which became an Air Command (rather than an army one). They swiftly opened up the entire country as they linked up their possessions in Egypt and Palestine with Iraq and India beyond. An early initiative was when the RAF was given the task of opening an air mail route across Transjordan. Traces of their work can still be seen in the Basalt Desert (Fig. 14.8B).

Finally, the uses and influence of the past in the landscape and life of modern Jordan should be touched on. Some sites are preserved by being used, others still by conversion into functioning components of the modern built environment (Fig. 14.9). Much however, not least of the recent past, is being swept away by modernization (Fig. 14.10A). The mud-brick tower houses and gardens of Ma'an are one striking example. Elsewhere, the past has been incorporated fully and continues to give form to the present (Fig. 14.10B).

Fig. 14.1B: Jiza: the reservoir and hajj fort overlooking it (APA 98/ SL11.24, 13 May 1998)

Darb al-Hajj al-Shami and Jiza

For over 1,200 years there was an annual Pilgrimage passing down through Jordan along one or other of the Hajj Roads. Over many centuries, probably several million people followed the routes in Jordan alone, on foot, on the backs of camels, horses, mules, donkeys or asses, or carried in a litter. In 1876 when Charles Doughty travelled with the Hajj through Jordan, he estimated there were up to 6,000 people and 10,000 animals, often walking or riding in parallel columns.

The Syrian Pilgrimage Road followed different alignments. For example, south of Amman one might follow a westerly route through Jiza **(Fig. 14.1B)** or a more easterly one through Dab'ah (Fig. 14.2). It can only really be viewed today where it runs through areas of undeveloped steppe or desert. It was provided with bridges in places but was not normally surfaced.

Tristram in 1872 wrote:

We might have been galloping across a deeply ridged fallow. For about a quarter of a mile in width, every three or four yards was a deep wide rut, all in parallel lines. We were crossing the hadj road. Files of hundreds of camels, slowly following each other in the weary tramp to Mecca, had, in course of ages, worn the hard surface of the desert into these deep furrows.

And Doughty soon after described 'a multitude of cattle paths beaten hollow by the camel's tread, in the marching once a year, of so many generations of the motley pilgrimage over this waste'.

In this area south of Qasr Mshatta (Fig. 12.1) (including under the modern Queen Alia Airport terminals), is the trace of a partly sunken trackway, presumably the 'hollow' track reported by Doughty. The type is common around the world where routes are unsurfaced and become worn away to a considerable depth. It runs in generally straight lines and in a broadly north–south alignment **(Fig. 14.1A)**. There are gaps but it can be followed for several kilometres and finally runs out just a few kilometres northwest of Qasr Dab'ah (Fig. 14.2). This is surely the Hajj Road though it may be following an earlier route from Roman if not Nabataean times.

The importance of water was recognized in 1835, when a report on the condition of the forts noted 'water on the pilgrimage route is the greatest necessity' (trans. Abujaber) and Doughty stressed the same point 41 years later:

The kellas [qal'at = fort] are fortified water stations weakly garrisoned; … The cisterns are jealously guarded; as in them is the life of the great caravan … The kellas stand alone, as it were ships, in the immensity of the desert, they are not built at the distances of camps, but according to the opportunity of water … (1926: 9)

Figure 14.1B shows the reservoir and hajj fort at Jiza. The place was settled long before Islam — there is a Nabataean and Roman settlement, and a Roman document of *c.* AD 400 locates a regiment of cavalry there; the reservoir is Roman if not earlier. However, the reservoir was re-used in the post-Roman centuries and is in fact the largest in Jordan — 128 x 100.5 x 5.3 m, capable of holding some 68,000 cubic metres of water. In this view we are looking southwest over the modern Desert Highway with the reservoir in the centre. The rectangular building on the high ground to its south is the medieval hajj fort as restored in the 19th century and now a Jordanian military post.

Fig. 14.1A: Darb al-Hajj al-Shami, looking north (APA01/SL23.25, 6 May 2001)

Qasr Dab'ah

Jordan has
mainly of the
of Amman an
Although it is
nearby, the ar
under cultivatic
now we conf
'stand[ing] alo
desert'. At the
would have ha
annual pilgrims

Almost all t
20–30 m on ea
In the middle i
Dab'ah has tw
rooms were fo
perhaps 10 or
on the north, b
lie two reservoi
side (with a m
filled by water c
graves to the
beduin ones, b
standard featur

Fig. 14.2A: Dab

Fig. 14.6B: Hejaz Railway: railway station at Ma'an (APA02.2/ SL24.9, 30 September 2002)

The Hejaz Railway

Between 1901–04 the Hejaz Railway was extended south of Damascus as far as Ma'an. It was a major undertaking — and a deadly one: in 1903–04 over 400 workers died of cholera building the stretch from Dera'a to Amman. The line itself, constructed by German engineers, meandered down through the hills north of Amman and round the city, then onwards, in increasingly straighter stretches in the more open steppe further south. Where it crossed wadis, great embankments were built and bridges constructed. A succession of railway stations was built at regular points in Jordan; in several cases they were located close to the hajj forts of the Pilgrimage Road. The buildings were simple — rectangular structures, usually two-storeyed and with a pitched tile roof of a type adopted from Anatolian vernacular architecture. The railway took over from the hajj forts and its sunken road. Instead of the massive logistical undertaking along a desert road, pilgrims, henceforth, could travel more directly and rapidly by rail and the era of the great annual trek was over.

One of the most impressive pieces of engineering along the line is in the eastern suburbs of Amman itself **(Fig. 14.6A).** There the engineers had to cross the deep and broad valley of the Wadi Marka, just south of the airfield (Fig. 14.8A). The solution was this superb two-storeyed viaduct, over 50 m long. Today it soars over a noisy four-lane highway, but the bright warm colour of the local Amman masonry gleams in the late afternoon sunshine.

Far to the south, at Ma'an, the railway station is still a relatively busy junction **(Fig. 14.6B).** The masonry buildings of the railway station and the accompanying water tanks stand out in their orderly rows, parallel to the line itself and accentuated further by their pitched roofs of red tiles. The large two-storey building (above centre) was originally the Railway Hotel. In recognition of its role in the Arab Revolt it has become a national museum, known as King Abdullah's Palace. The surrounding town has flat-roofed buildings — once commonly of mud-brick (Fig. 14.10A) but now largely concrete.

Fig. 14.6A: Hejaz Railway: viaduct near Amman (APA02.2/SL34.6, 2 October 2002)

Fig. 14.8A: Marka, looking north (APA99/SL11.34, 14 June 1999)

RAF Marka and the Airmail Route

By 1917 there were considerable numbers of Imperial German soldiers and airmen operating with the Turkish forces in this region. A key point in Jordan was Marka, 3 km northeast of Amman. There was a railway station there and by 1917 an airfield had been established on the plateau above, at which was stationed No. 14 Squadron of the Ottoman Air Force (but largely staffed by Germans). Old German photographs of 1917–18 show a military camp beside the railway station and a later aerial photograph of 1918 shows Australian air force bombs exploding around the station.

After 1919 the newly created British Royal Air Force took over the Ottoman/ German airfield as RAF Marka (assigning, coincidentally, No. 14 Squadron of the RAF). The British base of the 1920s–50s is still there **(Fig. 14.8A),** encapsulated inside the modern Jordanian military base and civil airport of Marka. The air photograph shows the site in 1999, with the red-tiled roofs of the Marka Railway Station in the valley below the camp. On the plateau can be seen the dark masonry buildings of the British camp with, still, barrack blocks with verandas, a cinema, canteen, Officers' Mess, offices, an outdoor bar overlooking the valley and ornamental garden in the form of a Union Flag. It is remarkably well preserved, a little piece of imperial Britain, accidentally saved.

The appearance of aircraft and their bases opened up the country dramatically, both for reasons of internal security and for reasons of wider imperial policy. Already, before World War I, Britain had important imperial footholds in Egypt and the Persian Gulf. After 1919, with Mandates over Palestine, Transjordan and Iraq, these possessions were linked and formed an obvious path towards the major possession, India. In 1926 the RAF was given the task of blazing a trail — literally — for a future airmail route from Heliopolis in Egypt, to Ramadi in Iraq, then on the India. Transjordan was barely established but the work went ahead rapidly.

Fig. 14.8B: Airmail Route Marker 23 (APA02.2/SL18.33, 29 September 2002)

The aircraft used were lumbering bombers, very slow and prone to engine failure. Navigation equipment was limited and Jordan lacked the roads and railway lines fliers could follow in Europe. The problem was resolved by one of those bold gestures imperial powers embrace. Aircraft could follow the first leg of their journey relatively easily from Egypt, through halts in Palestine to a landing at an airfield at Jiza 40 km south of Amman. This was a significant place — a Roman town and reservoir lay there, a Hajj fort (Fig. 14.1B), then a station of the Hejaz Railway and today the current international airport lies just on its east.

After Jiza pilots travelled with a route map that showed a succession of Landing Grounds at intervals of 15 to 30 miles, each marked by a large number inside a circle of about 20 metres diameter **(Fig. 14.8B).** To lay out the route, they mounted, in 1921, a combined survey on the ground and from the air, with armoured cars and trucks making a trail, guided by aircraft flying ahead to reconnoitre. The airmail pilots then followed this car track and where that was not clear, or it twisted, a furrow was ploughed with arrows to mark the way; ultimately the furrow was continuous.

Fig. 14.9B: Kan Zaman, Al-Yadudah (APA02.2/ SL33.36, 2 October 2002)

The Past in the Present ...: Ma'an and Kan Zaman

In every country traces of the past can be destroyed, damaged and ignored; the most prominent items can be taken into protection and marketed as archaeology for tourists. Some parts can be revived and put to use as functioning buildings. Two examples from Jordan are notable.

The dusty desert town of Ma'an has a very distinctive history. The important springs always made it an attractive centre for settlement and its geographical location made it commercially strategically important too. Some of this has been illustrated already (Fig. 14.7A). In the old town, one of the oldest buildings is the hajj fort (23.6 m square), dated to 1531. In the 20th century it became a prison but it has moved on again. As **Figure 14.9A** shows, the fort has been restored and the wider area landscaped. Today the building is an arts centre.

Thirteen kilometres south of Amman lies the hilltop village of Al-Yadudah **(Fig. 14.9B).** As we know from an ancient church inscription, it was in the territory of Philadelphia in Roman times; now it is being drawn physically into the orbit of sprawling modern metropolitan Amman. It was a well-known place already in the 19th century when travellers remarked on its ruins. Soon after, the Abujabers, a prominent family from Salt, bought land there and established themselves in what soon developed into a fortified village built out of ruins. In time they created accommodation for travellers and stables for their animals, to create a thriving enterprise close to Amman.

Today it has gone a step further — with parallels at other such sites in Jordan. The residential village and farming buildings have been transformed again. The centrepiece is a high quality restaurant, largely set inside the barrel-vaulted stables — the large square building to the left of the courtyard. In the courtyard itself are the mouths of three of the more than 300 hundred wells and cisterns reported around the village. The remaining buildings of the old village have been converted into shops and craft workshops. Collectively the enterprise provides a livelihood for some 200 families.

Fig. 14.9A: Ma'an: Hajj fort as tourist monument (APA02.2/ SL24.5, 30 September 2002)

Fig. 14.10A: Ma'an — mud-brick tower houses and gardens (APA02.2/ SL23.33, 30 September 2002)

… and the Future: Ma'an and Irbid

The past can shape the future as well. At Ma'an we see relics of the dozens of mud-brick tower houses and their gardens, which once thronged the oasis and drew the attention of foreign travellers. But many are now gone and the few remaining are vulnerable. **Figure 14.10A** shows a handful of gardens, outlined by irregular mud walls and packed with trees and crops. In three of them mud-brick towers can be seen still, though in others concrete houses are appearing. The land around is being cleared and, sadly, these old homes are likely to disappear as well.

In the northwest corner of Jordan lies the large city of Irbid **(Fig. 14.10B),** perhaps the ancient town of Arbela, which lay in the territory of Pella. It is much changed in recent generations but the distant past is still influential. In 1875 when Schumacher was there, despite its role as a centre of regional government, there were only 130 houses and *c.* 700 people. Originally the tell was *c.* 500 x 400 m, but flattening and modifications have made it lower and broader. The tell itself reamins the public heart, with its concentration of major public buildings. It is accentuated by and contrasted with a cemetry and densely-packed housing in the foreground and the more spacious suburbs and avenues beyond. Even so, Tell Irbid dominates the urban landscape, like an island rising up on the otherwise quite flat plain. A nice case of the past defining the centre and focus of habitation of a major city, through to the present, … and into the future.

Fig. 14.10B: Tell Irbid (APA02.2/ SL15.10, 29 September 2002)

PLACE-NAME INDEX

PLACES are indexed according to the principal element of the name, e.g. Wadi Mujib is under 'Mujib, Wadi'; Qasr el- Hallabat is under 'Hallabat, Qasr el-'. Numbers in **Bold** type indicate a photograph on that page.